# Great Creatures of the World

# WHALES

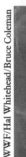

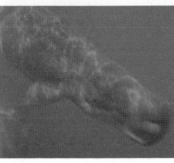
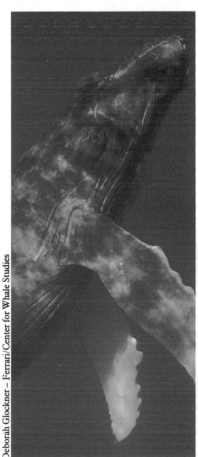

Francois Gohier/Ardea London

WWF/Hal Whitehead/Bruce Coleman

Deborah Glockner – Ferrari/Center for Whale Studies

*Great Creatures of the World*

# WHALES

## Facts On File

*New York • Oxford • Sydney*

Whales
A Great Creatures of the World book

Written by Lesley Dow

Consulting Editor: Professor M.M. Bryden
                   DSc FAIBiol
                   Professor of Veterinary Anatomy,
                   University of Sydney,
                   Australia

Adapted from material supplied by:

Dr Lawrence G. Barnes, curator and head, Vertebrate Paleontology Section, Natural History Museum of Los Angeles County, Los Angeles, California, USA

Professor M.M. Bryden, professor of veterinary anatomy, University of Sydney, Australia

Peter Corkeron, research assistant, Department of Veterinary Anatomy, University of Sydney, Australia

Carson Creagh, editor and natural history writer, Sydney, Australia

Dr W.H. Dawbin, honorary research associate, Australian Museum, Sydney

Hugh Edwards, marine photographer and author, Perth, Western Australia

Dr R. Ewan Fordyce, senior lecturer, Department of Geology, University of Otago, New Zealand

Sir Richard Harrison, Emeritus professor of anatomy, University of Cambridge, UK, Honorary Fellow, Downing College, Cambridge, United Kingdom

Kaiya Zhou, professor and dean, Department of Biology, Nanjing Normal University, Nanjing, People's Republic of China

Dr Victor Manton, curator, Whipsnade Park, Dunstable, Bedfordshire, United Kingdom

Dr Robert J. Morris, principal scientific officer, Institute of Oceanographic Sciences, United Kingdom

Marty Snyderman, marine photographer, cinematographer and author, San Diego, California, USA

Dr Ruth Thompson, author and historian, Sydney, Australia

Produced by
Weldon Owen Pty Limited
43 Victoria Street, McMahons Point, NSW 2060
Telex AA23038 Fax (02) 929 8352
A member of the Weldon International Group
of Companies    • Sydney • San Francisco
• Hong Kong • London • Chicago

Publisher: John Owen
Publishing Manager: Stuart Laurence
Managing Editor: Beverley Barnes
Project Coordinator: Claire Craig
Picture Editor: Kathy Gerrard
Designer: Diane Quick
Maps: Greg Campbell
Illustrations: Tony Pyrzakowski
Production Director: Mick Bagnato

Typeset by Keyset Phototype
Printed by Kyodo-Shing Loong Printing Industries
Printed in Singapore

10 9 8 7 6 5 4 3 2 1

*Page 1: Humpback whale mother and calf.*

*Page 2: The gray whale may look primitive but it is, in fact, the youngest whale species.*

*Opposite page: A southern right whale spy-hopping.*

# Contents

*Opposite page: A humpback breaching and showing off its throat grooves.*

# What are whales?

Whales are warm-blooded, air-breathing *mammals* that live in the sea. Many of them are toothless and use *baleen* (plates of horny fiber) to filter small *crustaceans* (sea animals with a hard shell or crust) and other small creatures from the water. They are sometimes called "great whales" because of their huge size.

The largest whale, the blue whale, grows to 100 feet (30 m) in length. It is the largest animal on earth. The smallest of the great whales is the pygmy right whale, which grows to 20 feet (6 m) in length. It is the same size as a great white shark.

It may seem hard to believe, but the ancestors of whales were hairy mammals that lived on land. About 50 million years ago some of these ancestors took to the water. Over millions of years they gradually lost most of their hair. Their bodies, limbs, internal organs, and five senses also adapted to life in the ocean.

Whales are found in all the oceans of the world. They are migratory, that is, every year they travel from areas of the ocean where they breed to areas where they feed. They are harmless to humans, but humans, unfortunately, have not always been harmless to whales. In many countries of the world the whaling industry used to kill thousands and thousands of whales every year. Whales are now protected from hunting, but many species have become rare in some parts of the world.

## "Sorting" whales

Scientists "sort" animals into different groups so that they can distinguish among them. An *order* is a large scientific group. Whales, as well as dolphins and porpoises, all belong to the order Cetacea, or cetaceans.

## Did you know?

The word "whale" is often used to describe all whales, dolphins, and porpoises.

However, some "whales," such as "white whales," "beaked whales," and "killer whales," are more closely related to dolphins than to great whales. They are only called "whales" because they are slightly larger than most dolphins.

You will find details of these "pretend" whales in another book in the series called *Dolphins and Porpoises*.

▼ *The humpback is easily recognized because it has very long flippers.*

Deborah Glockner-Ferrari/Center for Whale Studies

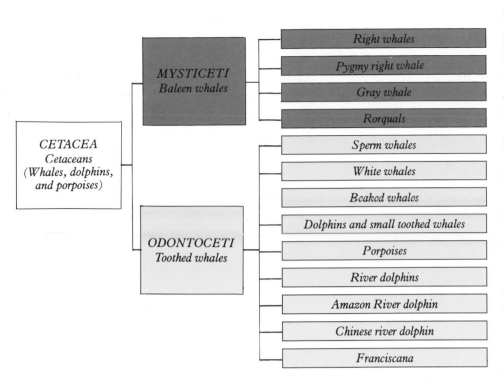

| ORDER | SUBORDER | FAMILY |
|---|---|---|
| CETACEA Cetaceans (Whales, dolphins, and porpoises) | MYSTICETI Baleen whales | Right whales |
| | | Pygmy right whale |
| | | Gray whale |
| | | Rorquals |
| | ODONTOCETI Toothed whales | Sperm whales |
| | | White whales |
| | | Beaked whales |
| | | Dolphins and small toothed whales |
| | | Porpoises |
| | | River dolphins |
| | | Amazon River dolphin |
| | | Chinese river dolphin |
| | | Franciscana |

the sperm whale, are baleen whales. The sperm whale is a toothed whale, it does not have baleen; it belongs to the suborder Odontoceti, along with dolphins and porpoises. But, since it is more "whale-like" than "dolphin-like" in size, it has been included in this book. You can read about the other toothed whales in *Dolphins and Porpoises*, another book in the Great Creatures series.

These two suborders can be broken down further into smaller groups called families. There are four families in the suborder Mysticeti and nine families in the suborder Odontoceti.

Each family contains one or more *genus*, and each genus contains one or more *species*, or kinds of whale. Only members of the same species can breed and produce offspring in their natural environment. The blue whale and the humpback, for example, belong to the same order (Cetacea), the same suborder (Mysticeti), and the same family (rorquals), but they are different species and cannot breed together.

The scientific name for a whale is made up of the genus name and the species name — like your surname and first name. The blue whale's scientific name, for example, is *Balaenoptera musculus*. Look at the checklist on page 67 to see the scientific names for whales mentioned in this book.

▼ *The blue whale (center) is the largest animal ever known on earth. The skeleton of an Odontocete or toothed whale is on the left and that of a Mysticete or baleen whale is on the right.*

This order is divided into two smaller suborders called Mysticeti (baleen whales), and Odontoceti (toothed whales). All of the whales we shall look at in this book, apart from

# Baleen

Baleen whales do not have teeth for feeding. Instead they have baleen or horny plates arranged on both sides of their long upper jaws. Baleen is similar to human finger nails or the outside of cows' horns; although it is sometimes called *whalebone*, it is quite different from bone.

The baleen plates are arranged like the pages of a book, with the parts facing the inside of the mouth frayed into bristle-like fibers. Whales use the baleen to sieve or filter out tiny animals, called *krill*, from the water. Baleen is obviously a very efficient means of catching food when you think how big whales can grow using only baleen to capture food.

The number of baleen plates varies according to species. Most whales have 200–400 baleen plates, but the gray whale has only 140–180 plates. The color of the baleen also varies from creamy-white through yellowish-white to slate-gray and blackish-brown.

Bowheads have the longest baleen — 15 feet (4.5 m) in length. Their upper jaws are arched so that the long baleen fits inside their mouths. Right whales also have long baleen, although it is only half as long as bowhead baleen. The baleen of other species is less than 3 feet (1 m) long. Some species such as the northern and southern right whales, and sei whales, have fine, almost silky, baleen. Other species have coarser baleen.

Unfortunately baleen was used by humans. *Whalers* slaughtered many thousands of whales, especially bowheads and right whales, for their valuable baleen as well as their oil.

▲ *Whalers killed thousands of whales for their valuable baleen, which they unloaded from the mother ships at port.*

▲ *The baleen plates are arranged like the pages of a book.*

◀ *Baleen provides a very efficient way for the whale to sieve or sift crustaceans (including krill) from the water.*

▲ *Krill are very small. The photograph here has been enlarged to show you what they look like. They are usually only 2–2½ inches (5–6 cm) long, but they are found in swarms large enough to provide a good meal for a whale.*

**Q.** What are krill?

**A.** Krill comes from a Norwegian word *kril*, which means "whale food." Krill are tiny shrimp-like crustaceans that live in Arctic and Antarctic waters. Although these waters are cold, they are rich in nutrients and the krill thrive there — that is until the large whales arrive to feed on them!

# Ancient whales

The history of whales goes back 50 million years. *Fossils* found in rocks, in various parts of the world, provide scientists with clues to the whales' past. Unfortunately there are gaps in the fossil record. Studying how whales have developed is like doing a jigsaw puzzle with some of the pieces missing.

## The original ancestors

The most likely original ancestors of whales were the mesonychids, which lived more than 50 million years ago in North America, Europe, and Asia. They were primitive, land-dwelling mammals that ranged from the size of a dog to the size of a bear.

Scientists believe that one of the smaller dog-sized mesonychids took to the water of the huge Tethys Sea, which stretched from what is now the Mediterranean Sea to India. This sea was a good source of food, and it seems that mesonychids living on the shores of the Tethys used to feed from its shallow waters. Gradually they began to spend more and more of their lives in the water.

The first mesonychids were probably a bit like otters or fur-seals, using four legs to swim in the water. They probably came back on to land to breed. Their eyes and ears adapted to water, and they lost their hair and developed *blubber* (a layer of fat between the skin and the muscles).

▼ *Mesonychids were the original whale ancestors although they looked more like wolves than whales.*

◄ *This is what* Protocetus *may have looked like.*

## Did you know?

Fifty million years ago, when the first whale ancestors were around, the map of the world looked different from the way it does today. Australia, South America, and Antarctica were joined together in one huge land mass called Gondwana. As Gondwana split up to form the continents we know today, new oceans were created. This allowed ancient whales to move to new seas and to develop new ways of feeding.

## Protocetus

The next stage in the evolution of whales is seen in *Protocetus* fossils 50 million years old. As you can see from the picture on the previous page, *Protocetus* looked slightly more like a whale than the dog-like mesonychid. Like whales today, *Protocetus* had a long slender upper jaw and a *blowhole* rather than a nose. It still had teeth and the remains of small back legs.

## Basilosaurus

When 28 giant *vertebrae* (small bones that make up the spine) were unearthed in Louisiana, scientists named the creature *Basilosaurus* — from the Greek *basileus* (king) and *sauros* (lizard). But it was not a "king lizard" or a reptile of any sort. It was a marine mammal — an ancient whale.

*Basilosaurus* bones, 38–45 million years old, have now been found as far apart as the United States, New Zealand, and Antarctica. These bones prove that at least some of the ancient whales had moved away from the area of the Tethys Sea.

About 50 feet (15 m) long, *Basilosaurus* weighed 11,000 pounds (5,000 kg). It had a mobile neck and a small head. The *flippers* were short and paddle-like but they also had an elbow joint, unlike the stiff, unbending flippers of today's whales.

It had back legs that were too small to be much use and it probably wriggled through shallow waters, possibly helped by *flukes* (the two triangular halves of a tail). *Basilosaurus* had a back fin (called a *dorsal fin*), a streamlined shape, and almost no body hair — just like whales today. The nostrils were at the top of the snout. It still had teeth and it probably ate fish.

## Primitive baleen whales

Whales today are different from their toothed ancestors. *Mammalodon*, a 24-million-year-old fossil found in Victoria, Australia, represents the link between ancient and modern whales. Although *Mammalodon* had teeth, they probably fitted together when the mouth was closed to form a sieve, like the baleen of today's whales. There may even have been baleen between its teeth. The bone structure of *Mammalodon's* jaws, the flippers, and also the throat grooves were similar to those of today's whales.

## Whales today

Whale families as we know them evolved from these ancient whales.

Right whales appeared 22 million years ago. Rorquals probably evolved about 15 million years ago. By 5 million years ago the humpback had appeared on the scene, though we still do not know why it should look so different from the other rorquals. The gray whale is the "youngest" of the living whales. It is only 100,000 years old!

Hopefully, scientists in the future will find some of the missing pieces of the jigsaw and so be able to complete the picture of the evolution of whales.

### Where did they go?

About 38 million years ago *Basilosaurus* and some of the other ancient whales disappeared. Perhaps these ancient whales disappeared, like the dinosaurs, because of some natural disaster — a meteorite striking the earth or volcanic activity. Many species were wiped out at this time but some, like the later ancestors of today's whales, survived.

▶ Mammalodon *looked more like a whale than any of the earlier whale ancestors did.*

# Kinds of whales

Whales come in all shapes and sizes, from the smallest, the minke whale, to the largest, the blue whale. In this chapter we shall look at the five whale families and the fourteen species of whale.

◄ *This gray whale looks very large looming below the surface of the water. It can grow to be as long as 50 feet (15.2 m).*

Jeff Foott/Survival Anglia

▼ *Whales are huge animals! As you can see they are many times the size of a human being.*

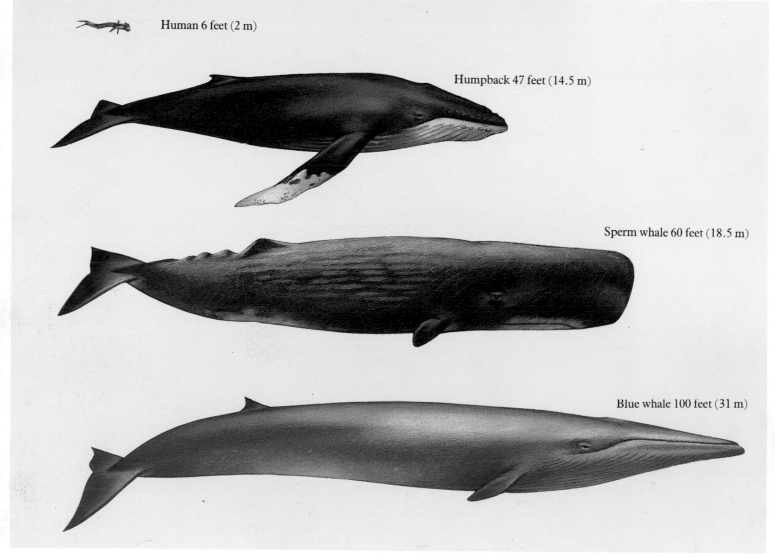

Human 6 feet (2 m)

Humpback 47 feet (14.5 m)

Sperm whale 60 feet (18.5 m)

Blue whale 100 feet (31 m)

## Right whale family

Right whales got their name because they yielded large quantities of oil and have long silky baleen. They were the "right" whales for hunters and whalers to catch. Right whales are large and heavy bodied. They have no dorsal fin, and their mouths are very arched to contain the long baleen.

## Southern and northern right whale

A southern right whale (shown here) and a northern right whale look very similar. They both grow to 58 feet (17.7 m) long, are slow swimmers, and both species are fat. The main difference between them is where they live. Southern right whales live only in the Southern Hemisphere, while northern right whales are found only in the Northern Hemisphere.

They have skin thickenings called *callosities* on their jaws and above their eyes. Lice and barnacles often attach themselves to these callosities. (You can see these in the picture.) The callosity on the ridge along the upper jaw is called "the bonnet."

Their flippers are spade-shaped, and their flukes are narrow and pointed. Older whales are darker than younger ones. The white patches you can see on the belly are where skin has been shed.

► *Southern right whale*

▼ *The southern right whale is found only in the Southern Hemisphere.*

Dave Watts/Australasian Nature Transparencies

15

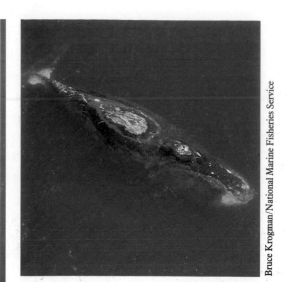

▲ *You can see the white chin and belly markings on a bowhead whale when it swims upside down.*

## Bowhead

This whale has a barrel-shaped body and an enormous head. As you can see from the picture, the flippers are small and shaped like paddles. The flukes are pointed.

Most bowheads are blue-black in color when they are young. They change to a blue-gray color when they are older. They are the only whales with a white chin patch, which can be seen when they swim upside down. A bowhead is 11–18 feet (3.5–5 m) at birth and grows to 60 feet (18 m) in length.

◄ *Bowhead*

## Did you know?

The bowhead has longer baleen than any other whale. At 15 feet (4.5 m) it would be twice the height from the ceiling to the floor in most modern houses, although getting the whale into the room of a house to test this would be impossible!

The bowhead's baleen hangs down from the arched upper jaw into the great mouth. Through it the bowhead strains some of the sea's smallest prey — imagine how these tiny crustaceans feel when they see this huge baleen about to engulf them.

## Pygmy right whale family

The only information we have on this family comes from 40 strandings off Australia, New Zealand, and South Africa.

### Pygmy right whale

A pygmy right whale, unlike its larger "cousins" in the right whale family, has a dorsal fin. However, it has no ridge on the upper jaw, and it is also much smaller. It grows to only 20 feet (6 m) in length and 4.5 tons in weight — small by whale standards but still large by our standards.

A pygmy right whale's flippers are small and rounded. Its flukes are broad, and it has two deep throat grooves. The dark gray on the back fades to lighter gray on the belly.

▲ *Pygmy right whale*

Marty Snyderman

▲ *The flukes of this gray whale are so large that they make the diver look tiny.*

# Gray whale family

This species is the only survivor of the "youngest" whale family. Only 100,000 years old, the gray whale family has been around for the same length of time as modern humans.

### Gray whale

A gray whale's head looks rather clumsy. It still has some hair left on its upper jaw. Instead of a dorsal fin, the gray whale has about ten small bumps on its back near the flukes, which are triangular. Despite their awkward-looking shape gray whales are able to swim faster than right whales.

A gray whale is a blotchy gray color but it often has yellowish patches of lice and barnacles on its head and back. It has two short throat grooves or pleats. It is the only whale that eats bottom-dwelling crustaceans. It must eat a lot of them because it grows to 50 feet (15 m) long and can weigh up to 33 tons.

► *Gray whale*

### The longest journey

Did you know that the longest migration of any mammal is the 6,000-mile (9,600 km) journey of the gray whale? Every October when the breeding season begins, this whale packs its bags and sets off from Alaska. Traveling at a speed of 4–5 knots it reaches Baja California in Mexico around January. It stays there for a few months to breed in the warm Mexican waters.

Don Croll

► *This gray whale seems to have no fear of people.*

# Rorqual family

This family contains the largest of all whales — the blue whale — and also one of the smallest whales — the minke.

All the species in the rorqual family have a similar shape. They are very streamlined, with pointed heads. They all have a small pointed dorsal fin, pointed flippers, and they are all fast swimmers. The throat grooves or pleats, which start under the chin and go along the belly, clearly distinguish this family from other families.

## Blue whale

This is the largest animal ever known on this planet — larger even than a dinosaur! It can grow to more than 100 feet (31 m) long, and one has been weighed (piece by piece so as not to break the scales!) at 180 tons. Its heart is the size of a small car, and its mouth is almost 20 feet (6 m) wide.

It is blue-gray in color with light gray spots, but its belly looks yellowy because cold-water algae (aquatic plants) live on it.

## Fin whale

The fin whale is the second largest whale and grows to 85 feet (26 m) long. Its back is usually dark gray to brown, and the belly is white. The right side of the jaw and the right baleen plates are white, while those on the left are dark. A fin whale can have as many as 100 throat grooves. It eats small fish such as mackerel, herring, and squid as well as crustaceans.

## Sei whale

This is the fastest whale in the sea. It "cruises" at 10–12 miles (16–20 km) an hour. It has a long slender muscular body, but for such a fast swimmer it has surprisingly small flukes. It uses its speed to chase schools of fish such as anchovies, herring, and sardines.

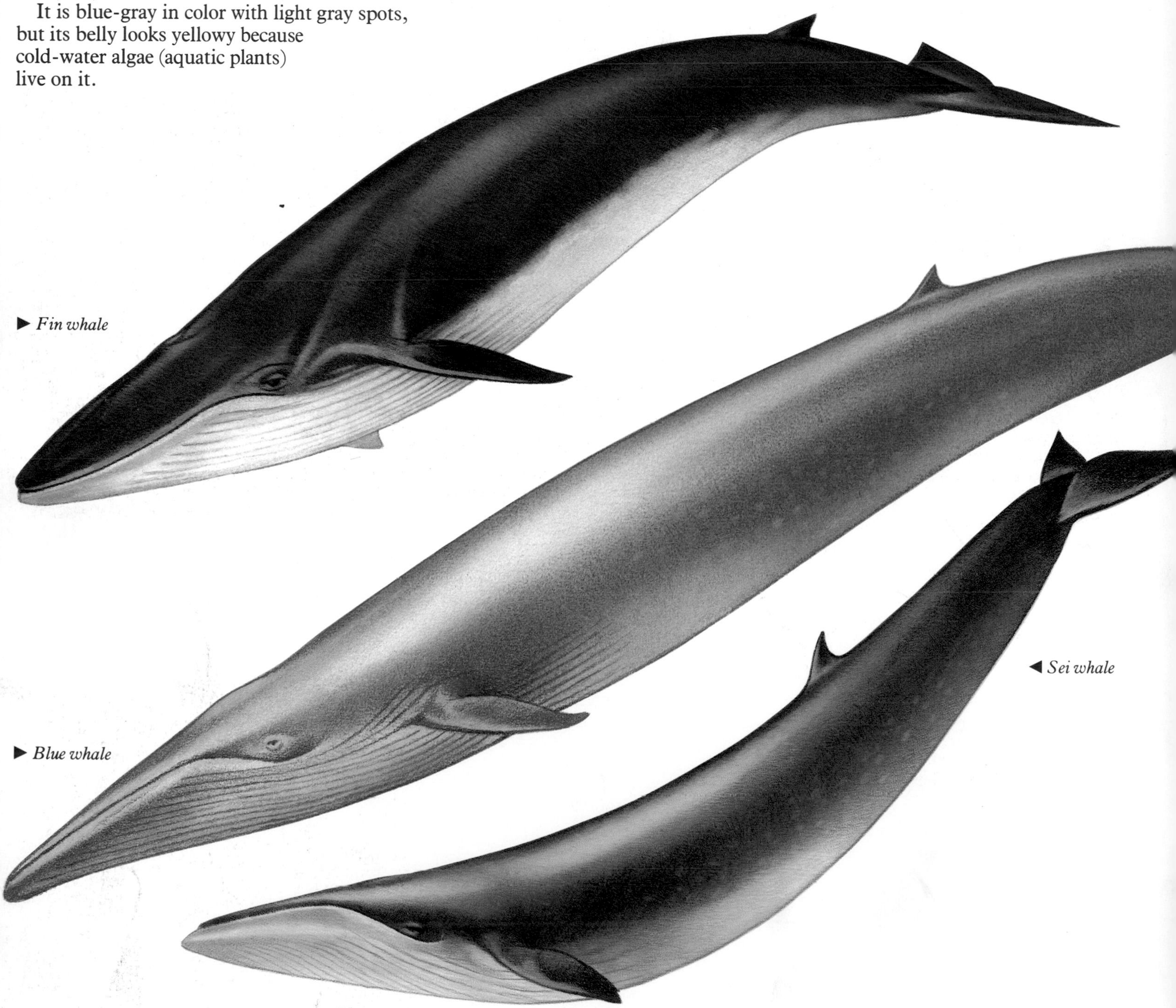

► *Fin whale*

► *Blue whale*

◄ *Sei whale*

## Bryde's whale

Unlike the other rorquals, this whale prefers warmer water and has a second ridge on each side of the central ridge on the upper jaw.

Bryde's whale is dark gray on its back with a lighter belly. The circular scars sometimes seen on its back are from attacks by cookiecutter sharks. It is a medium-sized whale. Calves are 14 feet (4.3 m) long and weigh 2,000 pounds (900 kg) at birth. Adults grow to 48 feet (14.6 m) and 20 tons in weight.

## Minke whale

This is the smallest species in the rorqual family — 30 feet (9 m) in length. Minke whales travel right into the pack ice at both poles to feed on herring, cod, squid, and krill. Most minke whales have a distinctive white band across each flipper and around the middle of the back.

◀ *Bryde's whale*

▶ *Bryde's whale has about forty or fifty throat grooves, which you can see here in the picture. This whale is skimming through the water with its mouth open to catch small fishes and squid.*

Bernie Tershy and Craig Strong/Earthviews

▶ *Minke whale*

▶ *A minke whale, the smallest species in the rorqual family.*

Robert Pitman/Earthviews

19

## Humpback

This whale is the best known and most studied of all the large whales. Its distinctive flippers are very long — up to one-third of its body length. (Its genus name is *Megaptera*, which means "great wing.") The flippers are bumpy at the front edge. The shape of its dorsal fin is quite different from the fins of other rorquals.

Its head is massive, and the lumps you can see in the picture contain hair follicles (small cavities from which hairs grow) and provide sites where barnacles and whale lice may attach. Humpbacks feed on krill and small fish only in cold water. They do not seem to eat in their summer breeding grounds. Despite giving up food for so much of the year, they grow more than 40 feet (12 m) long. Females are slightly larger than males.

◀ *Humpback whale*

Dean Lee

▲ *Humpbacks lunge at each other in a fight.*

▼ *Humpbacks feed only in cold water, and eat little or nothing in their warm-water breeding grounds.*

Colin Monteath/Hedgehog House, New Zealand

# Sperm whale family

The species in this family vary greatly in size but they have some features in common. The top of the head is blunt and extends much farther than the tip of the narrow lower jaw. The lower jaw fits into a groove-like channel and contains the teeth. In the front of the head, above the upper jaw, there is a *spermaceti organ*, which contains a special wax-like substance that is different from the oil of the baleen whales.

All species are deep divers and feed on squid. They have only one blowhole, unlike baleen whales, which have two. The dwarf sperm whale is not a well-known species and there is no picture of it here.

## Sperm whale

Sperm whales are the deepest divers of all the whales. A male sperm whale can grow to 59 feet (18 m) and weigh up to 45 tons. Females are smaller — 39 feet (12 m) long.

A sperm whale has no dorsal fin. Instead it has a series of bumps along its back toward the flukes. The first bump is often large and triangular. The light brown to blue-gray skin is rippled on the back and sides. A sperm whale has 18–25 large teeth on each side of the lower jaw, and these teeth fit into sockets in the upper jaw.

## Pygmy sperm whale

Unlike its larger cousin, the pygmy sperm whale has a small fin. There is no difference in size between males and females, both grow to 12 feet long (3.7 m) and weigh up to 880 pounds (400 kg). A pygmy sperm whale has 10–16 long, curved, sharp teeth in the lower jaw, which it uses to eat squid, octopus, small fish, and crabs.

▶ *Pygmy sperm whale*

▶ *Sperm whale*

## A white whale!

When we think of whales we think of large gray or black mammals. But did you know there have been sightings of white sperm whales? One whaling story from the nineteenth century tells of a white sperm whale, called Mocha Dick, which used to attack whaleboats in the eastern North Pacific. Perhaps the famous story of Moby Dick, a fiery but storybook white whale, was inspired by the adventures of this rampaging whale.

# How do whales eat?

Most baleen whales feed on large numbers of very small shrimp-like crustaceans and copepods. Dense swarms of these crustaceans are found in the upper layers of very cold waters. The whales skim through this food with their mouths open, taking in tons of water. They clamp their mouths closed, and the water filters out through the baleen plates. The tiny crustaceans are left trapped behind the bristly baleen.

### Throat grooves
Some of the rorquals, especially the blue whale, are huge creatures. They grow to be this big on a diet of very small crustaceans, so they need to take in huge amounts of water to filter enough crustaceans to keep them alive. To help with this, all rorquals have grooves or pleats in their throats. These extend from under their chins to well past the flippers. The grooves allow the throat to expand like the pouch-like sack of a pelican.

### Bottom feeding
Gray whales are the only whale species to "plow" or stir up the seabed with their snouts.

They then suck the muddy water into their mouths to leave the tiny crustaceans and fish trapped in the baleen. As most gray whales stir up the bottom with the right side of the mouth, the baleen on that side is often worn down.

### Bubble netting
Humpbacks use a number of feeding methods, but the most unusual is called "bubble netting."

A humpback swims in a circle below a large swarm of krill. As it circles and rises slowly toward the surface, it blows out air, which rises as bubbles to the surface. A chain of these bubbles gradually forms a net or screen around the krill. The humpback then comes straight up out of the water inside the net of bubbles to engulf all the helpless krill trapped there.

### The toothed whale
Sperm whales have teeth and, therefore, have a different diet from the other whales. They dive very deep to find giant squid — their favorite food. The giant squid grows to 40 feet (12 m) in length, so it is almost as large as the sperm whale itself. Baleen would not be much use for eating squid !

▼ *Humpbacks feed in a number of different ways and often feed together in groups.*

◄ *Gray whales are the only whale species to feed on the sea bottom. They also feed on small crustaceans attached to seaweed.*

## Did you know?

Humpbacks have a number of different feeding methods. Sometimes they feed in groups, when as many as four to six whales herd schools of fish or shrimp. When they have "rounded up" the herd, the humpbacks then take turns to dive and lunge upward, with their mouths wide open, scooping up the prey.

▲ *Giant squids are sometimes almost as large as the sperm whales that feed on them.*

▲ *As a humpback rises slowly toward the surface, it sometimes blows out air, which forms bubbles. This is called "bubble netting" and it is used by the humpback to trap krill.*

23

# Where are whales found?

Whales are found in all oceans of the world. They also migrate, sometimes thousands of miles, every year.

### Hot and cold

Most whales spend the winter in warm-water breeding grounds. In summer they migrate to cold waters to feed. The map on this page shows you where these warm and cold water areas are. The coldest waters are found near the poles. In summer they are rich in krill, which are the main source of food for many whales.

Moving toward the equator from these coldest waters, the water temperature rises until you reach the warmest, tropical, waters around the equator.

### Northern Hemisphere whales

Bowheads, northern right whales, and gray whales are found only in the Northern Hemisphere.

Bowheads feed and breed in Arctic and subarctic waters and migrate according to the seasonal changes in the Arctic ice cap. Northern right whales are not found as far north as bowheads. But they migrate much farther south to breed in warm temperate waters off Florida and North Africa.

Gray whales feed in cold temperate or subarctic waters in the North Pacific in summer. When the breeding season comes around in winter, they migrate long distances from Alaska, along the west coast of North America, to lagoons in Baja California in Mexico. There they breed in sheltered, warm, and fairly shallow water.

Rosemary Chastney/Ocean Images, Planet Earth Pictures

### Do they ever meet?

Whales that are found in both the Northern and the Southern hemispheres never meet or breed together. Their migrations are timed so that they are in the breeding grounds at different times.

### Southern Hemisphere whales

Southern right whales and pygmy right whales are found only in the Southern Hemisphere. Southern right whales are found in the South Pacific, Indian, and Atlantic oceans. Like their "cousins" the northern right whales, they breed in warm temperate waters. There is a big gap across subtropical and tropical waters between the two species, however (look at the map below).

Pygmy right whales are not a well-known species. They breed in warm temperate waters off Australia, New Zealand, and South Africa. But they may migrate into subantarctic waters to feed.

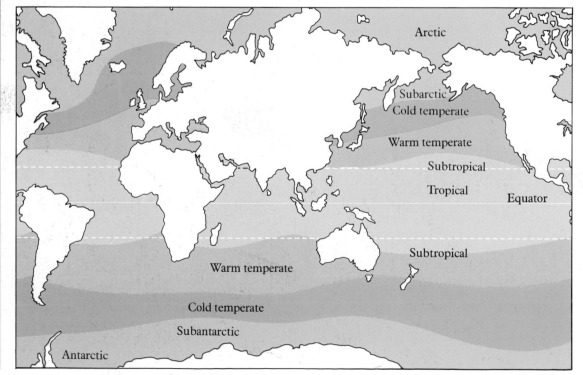

◄ This map shows water temperatures in the world's oceans. Whales feed in the cold waters (blue or turquoise on the map) and breed in warmer waters (pink or orange).

► Minke whales feed in extremely cold waters surrounded by ice.

**Q.** Do whales ever change their migration routes?

**A.** Humpback whales were unknown off Hawaii in the early nineteenth-century whaling days. Now it is the best-known meeting point and research center for humpbacks in the North Pacific. This is the only case where we know definitely that migration routes have changed.

## Worldwide whales

All other whale species are found in both Northern and Southern hemispheres.

Blue whales swim in all oceans of the world. Blue whales and fin whales avoid shallow waters, even when they migrate.

Sei whales seem to "feel the cold" more than other species. They do not travel so far north or south into the icy Arctic and Antarctic waters to feed, and they breed in the warmest tropical waters. They stay in deep water away from the shore.

Bryde's whales breed in the warm and subtropical waters of the Pacific, Atlantic, and Indian oceans. They do not migrate very far from these waters to feed. They are seen close to land, since they feed on coastal fishes such as herring and anchovies.

The minke whale travels right into the pack ice to feed. It migrates to warm waters to breed and can be seen surfacing in both deep and shallow waters.

Humpbacks migrate farther than any other whales. They breed in tropical waters but feed in Arctic and Antarctic waters. If you look at the map you will see how far they travel. Humpbacks are often found in shallow waters, which makes studying them easier.

Sperm whales are found in all oceans except the ice fields of Arctic and Antarctic waters. They too migrate long distances, especially the largest bull sperm whales. Sperm whales usually live in very deep waters but they have been known to *strand* if they do stray into shallow water.

Pygmy sperm whales are seen very rarely. They prefer tropical and warm waters. Dwarf sperm whales are among the least-known whales and are thought to live in deep water far from shore.

If you are ever lucky enough to see a whale, you might be able to guess which species it is according to the time of year, and the temperature and depth of the water.

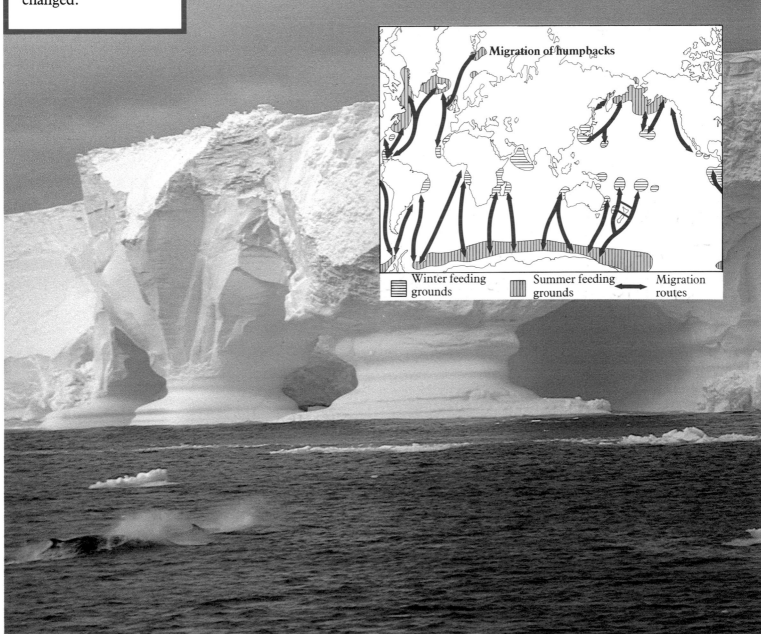

**Migration of humpbacks**

Winter feeding grounds | Summer feeding grounds | Migration routes

Paul Ensor

25

# Whale acrobatics

As well as coming up to breathe, whales sometimes make more dramatic appearances at the surface of the water.

## Spy-hopping

When a whale holds its body vertical in the water with its head peering above the water, it is said to be "spy-hopping." Minke whales often spy-hop between ice floes, and right whales have been seen spy-hopping in Arctic and Antarctic waters. Whether the whales have just popped their heads up to have a look around or to surprise a passing boat, nobody knows.

## Breaching

When a whale breaches, its whole body rears out of the water as it leaps into the air. It is an awesome sight. Most baleen whales breach, but the humpbacks breach more often . . . and are more athletic than most.

Humpbacks will even perform backward somersaults in the air before crashing back into the water. They breach most often near their breeding grounds when other humpbacks are around but sometimes a solitary animal will breach.

Perhaps whales breach to warn off other whales, to let others know they are there . . . or just for the fun of it!

Francois Gohier/Ardea London

▲ *This spy-hopping humpback looks as if it is doing the breast stroke.*

Francois Gohier/Ardea London

▶ *A breaching humpback must be an amazing sight for any passing sailor.*

◀ *When a right whale spy-hops, you can see the barnacles that attach to the callosities. Small whale lice also attach to the barnacles, giving them their light color.*

# The body of a whale

Scientists know less about the whale's body than they do about other mammals; whales are not easy animals to study! In this chapter we shall look at how the whale's body is built, although we do not always know exactly why it is built this way.

### Streamlined bodies

Whales have streamlined bodies, shaped like torpedoes. They have little or no hair, and the ears, genitals, and mammary glands (breasts) are inside not outside the body. Their shape and the lack of hair or parts that "stick out" help whales to move very smoothly through the water.

### Flippers, fins, and flukes

The whale's flippers are like your arms. But they are flat and have no elbow joint. The whale cannot bend its flipper in the middle . . . nor can it put its elbows on the table. There are four or five "fingers" inside each flipper, but a whale has more little bones in each flipper than you have.

▼ The humpback's flippers look more like arms than the small flippers of other whale species.

— (tip to tip) — 15 feet (4.5 m) —

**Flukes** (to scale)

Blue whale

Right whale

Humpback

Gray whale

Sperm whale

Mike Osmond

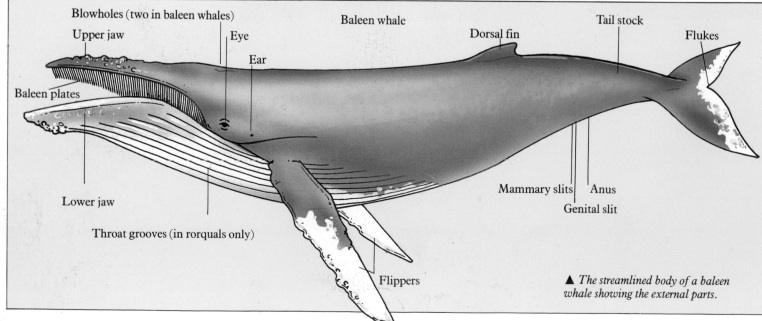

Blowholes (two in baleen whales)

Upper jaw

Eye

Ear

Baleen whale

Dorsal fin

Tail stock

Flukes

Baleen plates

Lower jaw

Throat grooves (in rorquals only)

Flippers

Mammary slits

Anus

Genital slit

▲ The streamlined body of a baleen whale showing the external parts.

Flippers come in all shapes and sizes. The pygmy right whale has tiny rounded flippers, but the humpback has long, slim flippers. Sometimes the humpback waves one of these flippers in the air. The flippers are used to help the whale steer and keep its balance.

The dorsal fin, on the whale's back, also helps with steering. The size, shape, and position of the fin varies. There is no bone in the fin, and it is held upright by tough fibers inside. Some species, like the sperm and gray whales, have humps instead of a fin, but two species — the bowhead and the right whale — have no fin or hump at all.

The flukes are horizontal. They beat up and down to move the whale through the water. The flukes have tendons and bundles of fibers to keep them stiff and they remain stiff long after the whale is dead.

## The head and skull

Baleen whales have a flat head above the eyes, that is, they do not have a forehead.

A whale's skull is "telescoped" or pushed in from the front to the back. Parts of the skull overlap just like the sections of a folding telescope.

This telescoping means that the upper jaw is pushed back under the eyes so that there is a very large roof in the mouth of a whale.

## The jaw and mouth

The lower jaw contains no teeth (except for the sperm whale) or baleen. The long upper jaw carries the row of baleen plates.

In right whales, especially in bowheads, the baleen is so long that the mouth arches in an upside-down smile to cover it. Rorquals have short baleen, and the mouth is flatter.

▼ *Whales' flukes come in many shapes and sizes but all are efficient means of swimming.*

Francois Gohier/Auscape

Q. Can whales smile?

A. The arched lower lip makes whales look as if they are smiling. But whales cannot smile. Indeed, they cannot make faces — sad or happy — like you can. This is because the blubber in the head prevents the muscles of the face from reaching the surface. So even if a whale was smiling on the inside, the "smile" would not show on its face.

▶ *This gray whale may look as if it is smiling but its expression always stays the same.*

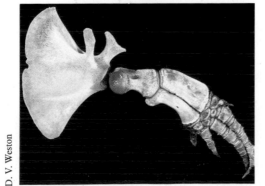

D. V. Weston

▶ *The bones inside a whale's flipper. Each "finger" contains many small bones.*

### Eyes, ears, and blowholes

Whales have relatively small eyes in large heads. The eyes are on the sides of the head just behind the gape of the mouth. Whales have no eyebrows to raise or eyelashes to flutter, and perhaps that is why their eyes seem to have no expression.

Like all mammals, whales have three tiny bones in the middle ear. But they have no visible ears. The ear canal, from a small hole just behind the eye, is usually closed.

Whales do not have noses. Instead they breathe through two blowholes on top of their heads. The sperm whale, like all other toothed whales, has a single blowhole.

### The whale's insides

Like you, the whale has a heart with four chambers. Like you, the whale has lungs because it breathes in the air when it surfaces.

It does not breathe underwater like a fish. It has a stomach, liver, kidneys, and intestines, but no gall bladder or appendix.

### The skeleton

The vertebrae are fused together in the whale's neck, so it cannot move its neck or turn its head. In most mammals, the bones of the pelvis support the back legs. Whales have no back legs and now have only the tiny remains of a pelvic bone.

The whale's ribs are delicate and are not attached very firmly to the spine or breastbone. When whales strand on land, the ribs are not strong enough to support the great weight of their bodies, and the chest often collapses. Like the outside of the whale's body, the skeleton is specially built for a sea-dwelling mammal.

▼ *The skeleton of a baleen whale.*

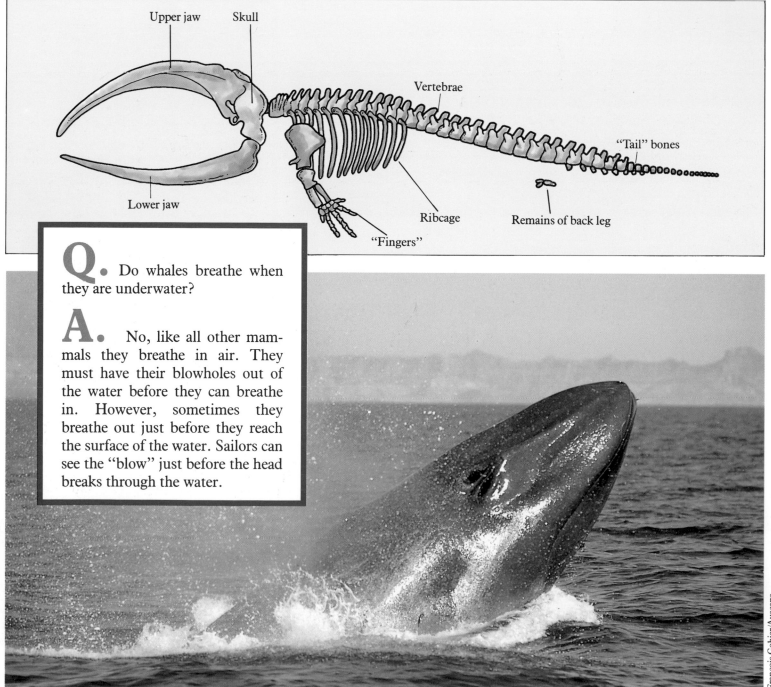

Upper jaw   Skull

Vertebrae

"Tail" bones

Lower jaw

Ribcage    Remains of back leg

"Fingers"

**Q.** Do whales breathe when they are underwater?

**A.** No, like all other mammals they breathe in air. They must have their blowholes out of the water before they can breathe in. However, sometimes they breathe out just before they reach the surface of the water. Sailors can see the "blow" just before the head breaks through the water.

# The blow

When a whale surfaces to breathe, it must first breathe out. The *blow* or "spout" is the name given to the cloud of moist vapor that is blown off as the whale empties its lungs.

The blow contains fine oil droplets from the whale's sinuses and a detergent-like substance from the lungs. It leaves a greasy film on anything it touches. Sailors in the whaling ships tried not to touch the blow. They said that it burnt the skin and caused blindness if it got into their eyes.

The blow smells like a mixture of bad fish and old oil. Whales have such bad breath that sailors once believed it could cause brain disorders!

The blow varies with the weather. It seems much whiter and can be seen more easily in cold weather. High winds can blow it in strange directions so that it no longer blows straight up in the air.

The blow also varies according to the size and species of whale. Experienced sailors can often recognize the species of whale from the blow. The blow of a sperm, blue, or fin whale can reach 26 feet (8 m) in height. Right, sei, gray, and humpback whales have a medium-sized blow of 6–10 feet (2–3 m). The minke whale blows to a height of only 3 feet (1 m).

How often a whale blows depends on what it is doing. If it is cruising undisturbed, a large whale blows out and breathes in once or twice a minute before diving for a long period. When it is being hunted, however, the whale breathes in less often.

By breathing out quickly and often while at the surface, the whale gets rid of the carbon dioxide and lactic acid that build up during a long dive. By breathing in, the whale gets the oxygen it needs for a dive.

Ben Osborne/Oxford Scientific Films

▲ *The blow is a combination of moist vapor, oil droplets, and a substance from the whale's lungs. It blows high into the air when the whale breathes out.*

British Museum (Natural History)

▼ *The sperm whale blow comes from its single blowhole. Whalers were able to spot the whale when they saw the blow rising from the sea.*

THE SPERMACETI WHALE

Francois Gohier/Ardea London

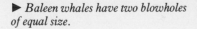

▶ *Baleen whales have two blowholes of equal size.*

# How do whales survive in the water?

The ocean is not an easy place to live, especially when your ancestors were warm-blooded, air-breathing land mammals. In this chapter, we shall look at how whales have adapted over 50 million years to life in the sea.

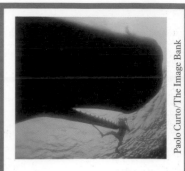

Paolo Curto/The Image Bank

## Changes to the body

Water is denser than air, and this means that it is more difficult to move in water. Can you remember how it felt the last time you waded through water?

Whales have a special streamlined body shape that helps to solve this problem. Although they are not related, a whale is more like a shark or a fish than a land mammal in shape.

Many whales grow to a large size. On land, where gravity is important, they would need four very strong legs to support their weight. But the whale's body is weightless in water. The whale has gradually lost its legs since it no longer needs them, just as you have lost the tail your ancestors had because you no longer need it. Whales now have flippers instead of front legs. They have no back legs and are propelled by flukes. Flippers and flukes are much more suitable for a sea-dwelling mammal.

## How whales swim

Water offers resistance to a backward force. (Think how hard you have to pull on oars to overcome this resistance and move a rowing boat forward.) Whales do not use a backward force when swimming. The whale's flukes beat up and down, not backwards and forwards. This is an efficient way for whales to propel themselves through the water.

Frictional resistance or "drag" also develops at the surface of the skin as a body moves through water. The whale's skin is silky smooth with no folds or pores. The head joins the body smoothly with no neck or shoulders. The body tapers smoothly into the tail. All of these help to reduce drag as the whale moves through the water.

▼ *The flukes move up and down to propel the whale through the water.*

**Q.** Which whale has the biggest head?

**A.** The sperm whale has a huge head. It contains the spermaceti organ, which is rich in oil. At the surface of the water the oil is usually liquid and may help the sperm whale to float. When the sperm whale dives into very cold waters the oil becomes solid and heavy, helping the whale to stay down.

David Rootes/Seaphot Limited/Planet Earth Pictures

G. L. Kooyman

▲ *Whales can keep warm even in icy waters since their bodies have adapted to cope with the cold.*

Tony Martin/Oxford Scientific Films

▲ *Blubber is a thick layer of fat that keeps a whale warm.*

Oily skin cells and a string of mucus from the eyes, which passes back along the body, also reduce drag. They even help the whale's passage through the water.

But the greatest help in swimming comes from the whale's flukes. The movement of the flukes creates a smooth layered flow of water over the whale's body. There is no turbulence (disturbance of the water) created between the water and the whale. This greatly reduces drag and allows the whale to reach great speeds with less effort.

### Keeping warm in a cold sea

Whales have a body temperature of 98.6° F (37° C), the same as yours. But they swim in seas that can be as cold as 29° F (−1.7° C). How do they keep warm in such cold water?

The huge size of whales helps them to keep warm. The rate at which heat is lost depends on surface area (the outside size). Surface area is less as body weight increases, so to keep warm in water, the bigger or heavier you are the better, since less heat is lost.

Whales also have a thick layer of fat or blubber under their skin. It keeps heat in like the insulation in the walls of a home. But there is no blubber in the flippers, flukes, or fins. On cold days your toes, fingers, nose, and ears (your extremities) feel the cold most.

Blood flow is reduced to these parts. By staying deep within the body, the blood remains warm, which it must be to permit normal functioning of the most important organs such as the heart and the brain. In extreme cold, however, the tissues of the extremities die from lack of blood flow. We call this frostbite. The whale has developed an efficient system of blood vessels to keep its extremities (flippers, flukes, and fins) supplied with blood.

Warm blood from the arteries, which are enclosed in bundles of veins, goes to the flippers, flukes, and fins. It warms up cold blood returning from those regions, and in doing so becomes cooler itself. In this way blood can continue flowing to the extremities and heat is not lost to the surrounding water.

| 98.6°F | ← | 73.4°F | 53.6°F | 42.8°F | ← | 39.2°F |
|---|---|---|---|---|---|---|
| 98.6°F | → | 77°F | 59°F | 46.4°F | → | 39.2°F |
| | ← | | | | ← | |

▲ *In the flippers, flukes, and dorsal fin, blood from the heart passes through the central artery at 98.6° F (37° C) and exchanges heat with the cooler blood in the veins on each side of it. This arrangement prevents too much heat being lost from the skin.*

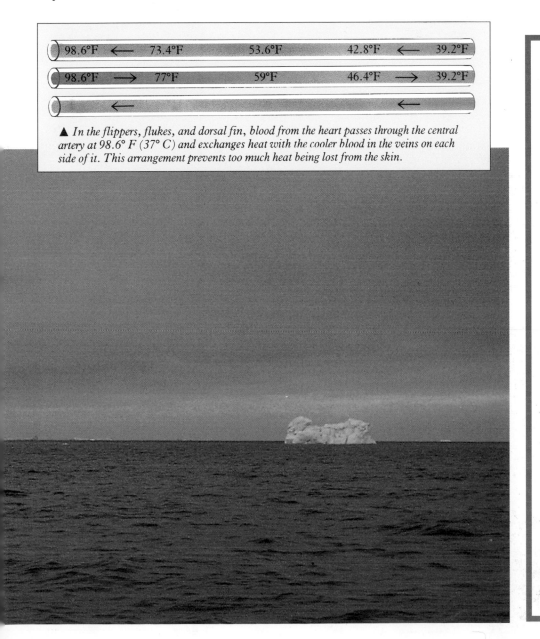

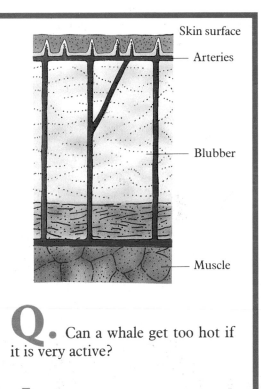

Skin surface
Arteries
Blubber
Muscle

**Q.** Can a whale get too hot if it is very active?

**A.** Blubber helps to keep a whale warm in cold water. It can also help to keep the whale cool. Large arteries run up through the blubber to the surface of skin. If the whale is "rushing about" a large quantity of blood is pumped through these arteries. The skin warms up, and the heat is lost in the cool surrounding water.

# Diving

All whales are skilled divers. The sperm whale dives deepest — up to 1.75 miles (3 km) deep — and stays down longest (up to 2 hours).

Have you ever choked and spluttered after breathing in water? Whales do not have this problem. The nasal passages to the blowholes are very twisted. The larynx opens into the nasal cavity rather than into the throat. And, of course, they close their blowholes before diving. All of these prevent water from entering the airways.

## Oxygen

Whales breathe less often than land mammals, but they take deeper breaths and take more oxygen from the air they breathe.

However, for their size, their lungs are no larger than those of land mammals. How then can they store enough oxygen to last during a long dive? The answer lies in the whale's blood circulation system and muscles. Whales seem to store and transport oxygen in their blood more efficiently than we do.

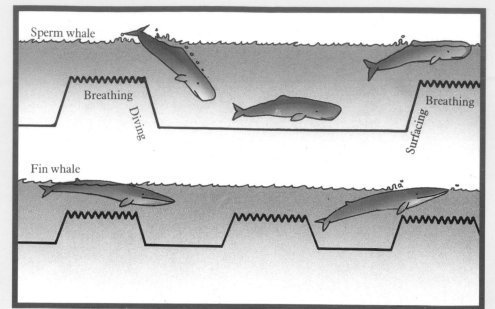

Sperm whale

Breathing

Diving

Breathing

Surfacing

Fin whale

▲ *The sperm whale dives deeper than the fin whale so it breathes less often but more rapidly than the fin whale.*

Mike Osmond/Pacific Whale Foundation

◄ *Whales hold their breath during a dive before coming up to the surface to breathe once again.*

▼ *Whales breathe more efficiently than we do since they take more oxygen in and empty more air out of their lungs with every breath.*

Francois Gohier/Auscape

▲ *If there was a whale Olympics, the sperm whale would win the gold medal for the deepest, longest dive.*

▶ *Whales have a very complex blood system including a large net of blood vessels behind their ribs.*

### Blood, blood, glorious blood

Blood makes up 10–15 percent of a whale's body weight, compared with only 7 percent in humans. Whales also have more of the oxygen-carrying red blood cells. And they have more hemoglobin (red protein that contains iron) in their blood and muscles than humans. This increases the amount of oxygen that the red blood cells can carry.

Whales, like many aquatic animals, may also redistribute blood during a dive so that only the essential organs get the scarce blood that contains oxygen. Blood flow continues to the brain and heart during a dive. But blood to the stomach, intestines, and kidneys may be cut off almost completely.

Unlike land mammals, whales are able to tolerate higher levels of lactic acid and carbon dioxide that build up when there is no fresh oxygen supply. This explains why they can stay underwater for so long without having to breathe out . . . or in.

### Pressure problems

Human divers use tanks of compressed air when diving. This air contains nitrogen, which dissolves in the blood and builds up during the dive. If the diver rises to the surface too quickly the nitrogen forms bubbles in the blood vessels and tissues. This is thought to be the cause of the "bends" that divers sometimes suffer from.

Whales can dive to great depths where the pressure is great. Why do they not get the bends like human divers do?

Whales take down their own air supply. There is only a small volume of nitrogen present in their lungful of air, and not enough to cause them to get the bends.

At great depths and at great heights, our ears pop as the pressure on the outside of the ears builds up. Whales have special sinuses in the lining of the middle-ear cavity. Under pressure, these automatically swell with blood and make the cavity smaller. This makes sure the middle ear is always at the same pressure as the outside water.

# The five senses

The ancestors of whales lived on land, and their five senses — seeing, touching, tasting, smelling, and hearing — were designed to work in air. When the first whales moved into the sea, their senses had to adapt so that the whales could survive in the water.

## Seeing

Light travels more slowly in water than it does in the air. It also refracts (bends) when it passes from air to water, so an eye that can focus in air cannot usually focus underwater. Human divers use diving masks underwater so that their eyes can focus in the pocket of air trapped behind the mask.

Whales do not need masks because they have developed strong muscles within their eyes. These muscles change the shape of the lens in the eye so that they can focus at the surface as well as underwater.

Whales are also able to see in the dark. The deeper the water, the darker it becomes. Whales' eyes have large pupils that collect the maximum amount of light. The pupils close to narrow slits when the whale is at the surface where the light is strong.

When looking at objects, a whale will sometimes turn on its side and look through one eye. The single eye can be moved around to give a wide range of vision. When focusing on closer objects, however, whales use both eyes.

## Touching and feeling

You touch and feel things with your fingers, hands, and sometimes your feet. Whales do not have hands or feet. They use their very sensitive skin to touch and feel. The skin of a whale contains a complex system of nerve endings. Some parts of the skin have more nerve endings and are more sensitive than others — for example, the head and jaw areas. Some whales may be able to use the skin around the jaw to detect vibrations in the water. They also sense pressure build-up in the skin around the jaw. This helps them to tell how fast they are swimming.

There are sensitive nerve endings in the skin around the blowholes. Whales can therefore "feel" when the blowholes are in the air and can be opened. One disadvantage of having soft sensitive skin is that it damages easily. Luckily, a whale's skin also heals fast. Older whales often have skin that looks battered and scarred by the many scratches and wounds they have received.

▶ *The head, jaw, and blowholes of a whale are very sensitive to touch and pressure.*

▼ *The eye of a gray whale.*

**Q.** Can whales see color?

**A.** Colors change underwater. Red or yellow light is quickly absorbed by water. Most objects appear blue-green in color. Whales live, mainly, in a world with little color and they probably have limited color vision.

◀ *The eye of this humpback has muscles to change the shape of the lens, and pupils that enlarge to see in the dark.*

### Tasting and smelling

Unlike sharks, whales do not have a very well developed sense of taste. However, they can possibly "taste" chemicals in the water, which may tell them if food, a predator, or another member of their species is nearby.

Whales cannot smell at all. They do not have smell receptors in the nose or a "smelling" system in the brain.

### Hearing

Whales do not have ears flapping on the outside of their heads. But the inner ears, middle ears, and ear canals are like those of other mammals.

Sound travels about five times faster in water than in air. An air-filled ear would be useless underwater. Whales, however, have a horny wax plug in their ears. It transmits underwater sounds to the inner ear. In the air, the wax plug probably makes them deaf.

**Q.** Are whales brainy?

**A.** Whales' brains are certainly very large. The cerebral hemispheres (the two halves of the brain) are like human brains. The cortex (gray matter) and the way it folds are more like the brains of cattle, sheep, or deer. Whales are large grazing animals. They are probably as intelligent as other large grazing animals such as cattle or giraffes. They are not as intelligent as monkeys, dogs, or dolphins.

▼ *Like all whales, this humpback has no sense of smell but probably has a little sense of taste.*

Rosemary Chastney/Ocean Images Inc./Planet Earth Pictures

# Parasites

Several creatures attach themselves to the skin of whales. Many of these are not true *parasites* since they do not gain nourishment from their hosts.

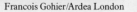

▲ *Whale lice are small crustaceans, quite unlike the lice we know.*

## Barnacles

Barnacles hitch a free ride for a meal by attaching themselves to the skin of whales. They eat small plankton and scraps left by the whales in the water around them. Often a crop of other stalked barnacles grow out of them. Changes in water temperature cause the barnacles to drop off.

## Worms

Parasites inside the whale are, of course, not easy to see. They include roundworms in the stomach, and tapeworms and thorn-headed worms in the intestines, lungs, flukes, and other organs. They do not seem to harm healthy whales, and it is unlikely that they would be a direct cause of death.

Francois Gohier/Auscape

▲ *The callosities or skin thickenings of this northern right whale are light-colored, partly because there are many whale lice attached to them.*

▶ *A barnacle, surrounded here by lice, feeds on a whale's scraps.*

Francois Gohier/Ardea London

## Lice

All whales have "lice." The lice, however, are not like the lice of land mammals. They are in fact small crustaceans. They cause little damage to the whales and, unlike barnacles, they are not affected by changes in water temperature. The lice gather around the eyes, flippers, and throat grooves. They are very easy to see on right whales where they gather on the wart-like callosities.

G.L. Kooyman

▲ *Lice gathered around the eye of a gray whale.*

39

# Birth and growth

Whales meet and mate underwater. Female whales give birth underwater to a calf that can only breathe in air. How do they do it?

**Male or female?**

It is very difficult to tell if a whale is male or female. The male's penis and the female's nipples are usually hidden inside the body.

However, if you look very closely at the belly of a whale you can tell which is which. The female has two tiny mammary slits, and the male's genital slit is nearer the navel.

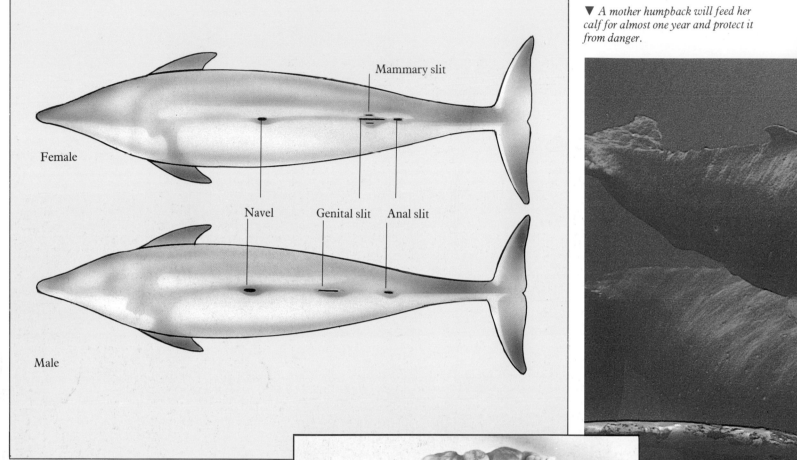

▲ The only way to tell a male and female whale apart is to examine the belly closely.

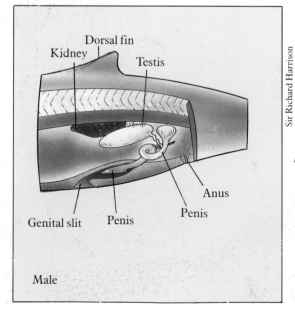

Sir Richard Harrison

▲ Scientists can tell how often a female whale has ovulated by counting the lumps on her ovary.

▼ A mother humpback will feed her calf for almost one year and protect it from danger.

**Male sex organs**

The penis lies inside the body and is held there by two strong muscles. The penis is made of tough, fibrous tissue. The testes (testicles) are also inside the body, just behind the kidneys.

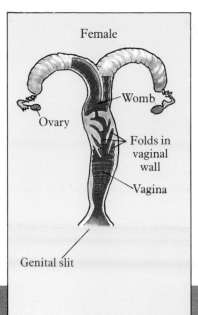

Female

Womb

Ovary

Folds in
vaginal
wall

Vagina

Genital slit

## Female sex organs

Female sex organs are similar to those of most female mammals. But there are one or two differences. The ovaries (where the eggs are stored) are very irregular in shape. They have lumps on them. After every ovulation (release of an egg), a white lump remains on the ovary. If scientists count these lumps they can tell how often a whale has ovulated.

There are a number of folds — like a series of funnels — in the vagina that point toward the womb. These folds may prevent water from reaching the womb where the calf grows before it is born.

## Mating

Mating in the wild has rarely been seen. Whales possibly mate in the same way as captive dolphins. The male swims up from beneath the female, and they mate with their bodies at right angles to each other. Mating takes only a few seconds.

**Q.** How old is that whale?

**A.** You can tell a whale's age from the wax plug in its ear. When the horny plug in the ear canal is cut lengthwise it has a pattern of layers. Light-colored layers of shed skin cells alternate with dark-colored layers of ear wax. Scientists count these layers to estimate age — it is lucky that whales do not clean their ears!

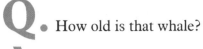

Mike Osmond/Pacific Whale Foundation

## Birth

Whales breed in warm waters during the winter months. The female is pregnant for 10–12 months. She has one calf every two or three years, and twins or triplets are very rare.

The calf is usually born flukes first, unlike most mammals, whose offspring are born head first. The birth is very quick . . . it has to be since the calf must surface for its first breath as soon as possible.

The mother may push the newborn calf to the surface to take its first breath. Calves are born with the instinct not to breathe until their blowholes are above the surface of the water.

### Feeding and caring for the calf

The calf is suckled just below the surface of the water. This means that mother and calf can breathe from time to time. A whale calf does not suck milk from the mother. The milk is ejected by the mother's muscles straight into the calf's mouth. This makes feeding the calf quicker . . . and safer.

The mother feeds milk to the calf for 4–11 months, and the calf begins to take solid food when it is less than one year old.

The mother protects her calf from danger and drives away intruders. Sometimes other females or "aunts" will help her to look after it.

The mother or possibly an "aunt" will sometimes support a sick calf at the surface so that it can breathe.

### Growth

The fetus (unborn calf) grows most at the end of the pregnancy. During the last two months, for example, the blue whale fetus puts on 2 tons in weight, which is approximately 72 pounds (33 kg) a day — up to a thousand times more than you grew just before you were born.

Whales produce milk that is rich in fat and, to a lesser extent, protein. Suckling calves, therefore, grow very quickly. A blue whale calf puts on 17 tons in weight — 176 pounds (80 kg) a day — when it is suckling. A calf that is 26 feet (8 m) long at birth may be 52 feet (16 m) long by the time it is only two years old.

The table below shows you just how much weight whales put on.

▼ *A 25-foot (7.5 m) blue whale calf can grow into a 100-foot (31 m) long adult.*

| ► This table shows how much weight whales put on between birth and adulthood. | Species | Length at birth | Weight at birth | Weight of adult |
|---|---|---|---|---|
| | Blue whale | 25 feet (7.5 m) | 2.2 tons | 150 tons |
| | Fin whale | 21 feet (6.5 m) | 1.8 tons | 70 tons |
| | Humpback | 14 feet (4.2 m) | 0.9 tons | 40 tons |

Ken Balcomb/Earthviews

▲ *If you look very closely you can see that this gray whale calf is being born head first. This is very rare since whale calves are usually born flukes first.*

# Getting together

Most mammals use their sense of smell to find a mate. But as whales have no sense of smell, they use actions to attract a mate.

Whales may chase, nuzzle, and nibble each other when they meet. These actions may be a friendly greeting between individuals and groups . . . a sort of kiss on the cheek. But they are also used to show that a whale is interested in a member of the opposite sex.

Sometimes courtship displays are more boisterous. Humpbacks, for example, roll over in the water, breach, or slap the surface with flippers or flukes. All these activities can show sexual interest.

Male humpbacks sometimes fight over females. These may be mock rather than serious fights . . . perhaps they are just trying to impress the female. But sometimes males will lunge at each other with their heads or hit each other with their flukes.

Since no one has ever seen humpbacks mating, we do not know how successful all their efforts are.

Dean Lee

▲ *Sometimes displays between male humpbacks seem to be very aggressive.*

Dean Lee

▲ *A humpback slaps the water with its long flipper to attract the attention of a mate — or perhaps to warn another male off its territory.*

Al Giddings/Ocean Images, Inc./Planet Earth Pictures

▲ *Humpbacks breaching together, possibly as part of their courtship displays.*

▶ *A humpback rolling in the water during courtship.*

Mike Osmond

43

# Family, friends, and foes

Whales, like many other animals, form groups. The members of the group "look after" each other, help each other with calves, and feed together. Sometimes they also fight.

### Male versus female

Groups are often all male or all female (except during breeding). That is because the interests of males and females are different. Males need to build up their strength to compete with other males for females to breed with . . . and to convince female whales they are the "best." Females, however, concentrate on making sure that their young survive. The strongest whale bonds are between mother and calf rather than those between "husband and wife."

### Nursery schools

Often the females will stick together as a group. This is common among sperm whales. Grandmothers, mothers, aunts, and calves stay in groups of between two and fifty in warmer waters while the males migrate to cold waters to feed.

These groups are called "nursery schools" and they provide protection for the young whales and calves. There have been reports of nursery schools of sperm whales keeping sharks and killer whales at bay. An injured whale, unable to swim to the surface to breathe, will often be assisted to the surface and supported there by other members of the social group.

### Harem masters

Bull sperm whales can be one-and-a-half times the length and three times the weight of females. The main reason for this is their different feeding pattern. Males migrate much farther than females to where there is more giant squid for them to eat.

When the breeding season starts, the males come to the nursery schools for mates. But they do not choose just one mate. The largest bulls fight for the whole group, and the winner becomes the *harem* master for the nursery school. Sometimes two bulls will combine and the two together will fight off other males.

Males stay with the harem probably for only a few days before moving on to the next female group — they are not very faithful !

### Bachelor schools

What happens when a whale is too big for the nursery school but not big enough to fight other bulls for a harem? Sperm whales join bachelor schools. The smallest males, who have just graduated from nursery schools, form groups of up to fifty bachelors. As the whales mature, group size gets smaller until, when they are about twenty years of age, the bulls are ready for a harem.

▼ *When a group of humpbacks gets together, boisterous behavior is common.*

R. & D. Keller, Australasian Nature Transparencies

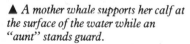

▲ *A mother whale supports her calf at the surface of the water while an "aunt" stands guard.*

WWF/Hal Whitehead/Bruce Coleman Limited

◄ *The bond between this mother sperm whale and her calf is very strong.*

A humpback whale will sometimes lie on its side in the water, lift its flipper in the air and gently wave it. The flipper, which can be up to 15 feet (4.5 m) long, may wave for as long as one hour. Who is it waving at? Do they wave back? Waving seems to happen in or near breeding areas, but what the wave means . . . we do not know.

M. Osmond

The amount of food available probably determines the size of whale groups. If food is plentiful a group can contain up to fifty whales. If food is in short supply, however, the group might be as small as between two and ten whales.

### Foes

Battles between bull sperm whales have been described by whalers who say that they seem to attack each other with their jaws. It must be an amazing sight to see such giants fighting. These fights are often more of a ritual that takes place during the breeding season than a real fight.

Humpback males fight over females. They lunge at each other with their throat grooves expanded — to make themselves look larger and more frightening. They hit each other with their flukes. Sometimes they slap the water with their long flippers. This releases bubbles in the water and may confuse a competitor. These fights can leave rivals with raw, bleeding patches on their backs and fins.

Despite the occasional fight, a whale has more chance of surviving if it remains with other members of the group rather than facing the dangerous ocean alone.

Al Giddings/Ocean Images Inc./Planet Earth Pictures

# The singing whales

Old-time open-boat whalers often told stories about "singing" whales and strange sounds that carried across the sea. But, nobody believed them. Whales have no vocal chords so people assumed they were mute.

Whale songs were first recorded, by accident, in the 1950s, when the United States Navy was operating sound equipment underwater. All that we know about whale songs has been discovered since then.

The blue whale makes loud moans lasting up to 30 seconds. These are the loudest sounds made by any living animal. Fin whales also produce long constant moans. Under certain conditions these can be heard for thousands of miles. Right whales, bowheads, and even the smallest minke whales also "sing." The only species of baleen whale that has not yet been heard singing is the sei whale.

The best singers of all are the humpbacks. They produce the longest, most elaborate songs of any whale . . . or possibly of any animal. Their songs are made up of a distinct sequence of different sounds. These sounds vary from groans, moans, roars, and sighs to high-pitched squeaks and chirps.

All humpbacks in the same area sing the same song. As the season changes so does the song. And each year's song is slightly different from the song of the year before. Humpbacks in different areas do not sing the same song, so humpbacks in the Caribbean do not sing the same song as those off the coast of Australia.

All humpback singers are male. They may sing to warn off other males or perhaps the best or more powerful singer attracts more females.

Humpback females do not sing to their calves — not even a lullaby! This is surprising since the bond between mothers and calves is so strong. However, some recordings have been made of right whale cows making sounds to their calves.

None of the singing whales would win prizes for tuneful singing, and their records would not reach the "top twenty." However, research into whale songs is helping scientists in their studies of whale behavior and migration.

▶ *A male humpback will sometimes sing even if he is alone with nobody to sing to.*

## Did you know?

Male humpbacks' songs last for up to 10 minutes. But they will repeat this song for hours at a time — like a record when the needle sticks. Although they sing most often in their breeding areas, their songs have also been heard during migration. Singing at their cold-water feeding areas is unusual — perhaps they need to concentrate totally on eating.

# The whalers of old

Whales have been hunted since people first appeared in the world. Our Stone Age ancestors used whale bones as rafters in their homes. Later peoples ate whales as well as shellfish. The occasional stranded whale provided food and many other useful products for our ancestors.

### The first hunters

The Inuit (Eskimo) people in single kayaks hunted whales and seals as soon as they learned how to make harpoons. But hunting large whales required a team effort. It also required a bigger skin-covered whaleboat — the umiak — since the kayak was too small.

In other countries, such as Japan and Scotland, men in rowing boats herded smaller whales and drove them onto land. The first people to hunt whales on a large scale were the Basques of northern Spain.

### The Basque whalers

In the twelfth century, Basque fishermen hunted northern right whales in the Bay of Biscay. The water here was deep enough for the whales but also close enough to land for the Basque fishermen to reach the whales in their small boats.

By the sixteenth century, the whales in the Bay of Biscay were very scarce. The Basques therefore built larger boats that could sail to the western North Atlantic as far as Newfoundland in search of whales.

Rose Bierce, Centre for Environmental Education

▲ *The Eskimo people of the Arctic made good use of any whale they caught. The Eskimo shown here is carrying a harpoon with two floats made from the air-filled intestines of a whale.*

▼ *A Stone Age rock carving from Norway with a whale in the bottom right-hand corner.*

University Museum of National Antiquities, Oslo, Norway

Mary Evans Picture Library

▲ *Dutch tryworks filled the air with smoke and the stench of blubber being boiled into oil. Tryworks on land were safer than tryworks on the deck of a heaving ship.*

## The Dutch whalers

The Basques taught the Dutch and others how to whale. In 1622 the Dutch built a whaling town at Spitzbergen, north of Norway. The town was known as "Blubber Town."

As well as the 18,000 men in 300 Dutch ships who hunted the whales at sea, there were hundreds more on land to boil down the blubber and provide food and supplies for the men on the whaling ships. Whaling was hard and dangerous work, but great fortunes could be made.

## The American whalers

Meanwhile, in the New World of America, whaling had also begun. Watchtowers were built at ports such as Nantucket, New Bedford, and Cape Cod. When right whales were sighted the boats took off from the shore after them.

One stormy day, a whaling boat was blown far from land, where it came upon a school of sperm whales. The crew killed one of the sperm whales and brought it back to land. They discovered that the sperm whale had huge quantities of oil, which could make them rich very quickly. The sperm whales and, later, the slow-swimming humpback whales became the new targets for whalers.

---

### Did you know?

The American whaling ships of the late eighteenth century had tryworks on their decks. The tryworks were brick ovens, used to melt the blubber into oil. The blubber was minced finely and forked into the try-pots. The crew then lit the fires (very carefully!) in the ovens. The blubber was boiled into oil.

---

► *Life could be hazardous for a whaler. These whalers have just been catapulted into the air by the whale's tail!*

▼ *Although sperm whales had no valuable baleen, they yielded far more oil than any other species so their oil was especially valuable. Here a catcher boat moves in for the kill, while the mother ship waits in the background.*

British Museum (Natural History)

Shelburne Museum, courtesy American Heritage/BPCC/Aldus Archives

## Technology and whaling

In 1864, a Norwegian whaler, Svend Foyn, invented a new harpoon gun. The gun was mounted in the bow of the *catcher* boat and could be moved quickly into position. It fired explosive harpoon heads. This piece of technology changed the face of the whaling industry and other advances in technology soon followed.

The catchers became faster and more manoeuvrable. The lines from the harpoon became longer and stronger. They were now wound on special engine-driven winches and run over a block so that the struggles of the whale would not break the line.

Machinery was installed to inflate the dead whale with air so that it would not sink to the bottom and decompose. The *crow's nests* that were used for whale spotting, were later replaced by planes and helicopters that guided the catchers to the whales.

Improvements in navigation and weather forecasting made whaling safer and more profitable. Radio beacons could be planted on a dead whale so that the catcher could move on to the next kill and come back later to pick up the dead whale. With the help of technology, huge numbers of whales were killed each year.

By the early twentieth century people became aware that many species of whale might be hunted until there were none left. Protection for whales was gradually introduced in most countries. Large-scale commercial whaling has stopped . . . at least for the time being.

The Whaling Museum, New Bedford, Mass

Mary Evans Picture Library

▲ *The soft iron of the harpoon head twisted inside the whale's body so that the whalers could get a good grip on the huge whale as they hauled it in.*

**Q.** Where did "thar she blows!" come from?

**A.** It was shouted from the crow's nest of the whaler. There was always a lookout, lashed by wind and rain, swaying wildly in the none-too-safe crow's nest. His job was to shout when he spotted the blow from the whale's blowhole. He was paid extra money for every whale he sighted.

▼ *Svend Foyn's invention of a harpoon gun mounted on the bow of the catcher spelled death for many whales.*

Mary Evans Picture Library

# Scrimshaw

Scrimshaw is delicately carved and decorated whalebone or teeth. Perhaps the name came from a Mr Scrimshaw, which would have been a good name for a scrimping second mate whose job it was to hand out supplies on board a whaling ship. The word might have come from "scrimshankers" (an old word meaning lazy layabouts) who did little work while the "real men" were at sea hunting whales. The Eskimos were the first to make scrimshaw. The European and American whalers copied them. There were many sailors on board the "mother ships" that looked after or "mothered" four or five catcher ships. If the ships were becalmed or ran into foggy weather there were often days, weeks, or months with little to do. To pass the time, many sailors carved scrimshaw. The technique was simple, but plenty of "elbow grease" was needed.

The tooth or piece of bone had to be cleaned, prepared, and polished. The sailors then used a jack knife, a sail needle, or perhaps a sharpened nail to engrave. If they were good at drawing they would etch the picture themselves. If they were not so artistic, they would paste a picture on the bone or tooth then trace the picture with the knife, nail, or needle.

After they had engraved the outline to the depth they wanted, they filled the lines in with lamp black (soot) or other colouring material. Finally, the scrimshaw was polished with wood ash until it shone.

Scrimshaw could be small or large, depending on whether a tooth, small bone, or larger bone (like the jawbone) was used. The sailors made ornaments, snuff boxes, "busks" for ladies' corsets, napkin rings, thimbles, buttons, brooches, riding crops, and sword-sticks. They made some of these items as presents for their wives or girlfriends. They also earned money by selling some when they returned to port.

The artists rarely put a name or date on their scrimshaw. They were obviously modest and did not realize that we would find the articles so interesting.

Most old scrimshaw is now in museums. Since whales have been protected, it is illegal to import or sell scrimshaw in most countries. The art of scrimshaw has now died out. But making the carving of scrimshaw illegal has done much to protect endangered whales.

Hull Fisheries Museum

▲ *Scrimshaw was made during whaling voyages, which could last for up to four years, for wives and girlfriends back home.*

Daisy Hayes/BPCC/Aldus Archives

▲ *An ivory pipe with scrimshaw decoration of Eskimo whalers.*

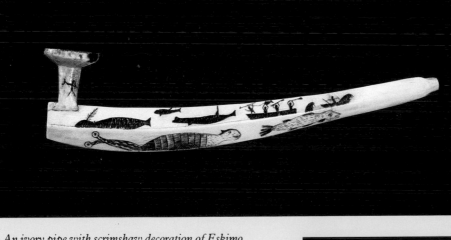

Jonathan Gordon/Seaphot Limited/Planet Earth Pictures

▶ *Carved in the shape of a sperm whale, this piece of scrimshaw shows a whaling scene.*

## Did you know?

Most scrimshaw now in museums was carved between 1830 and 1860. Since 1976, the Convention on International Trade in Endangered Species of Wild Fauna and Flora (CITES) has banned the sale or import of scrimshaw. So, if you find any scrimshaw in your home do not take it with you when you travel to another country — it may be confiscated if you cannot prove when it was carved.

# Using whales

Eskimos, American Indians, the Japanese, and natives of the Pacific Islands ate whale meat, long before European whaling started. It was a good source of protein for people who had poor soil, few crops, and almost no livestock.

Once the carcass had been stripped of meat, the hide and bones would also be used. The Eskimos, for example, used almost every part of the whale. Sinews, skin, and bone were used to build kayaks and homes. The air-filled intestines were used as harpoon floats.

**Baleen and blubber**

European and American whalers, however, did not hunt whales for food, but for the products they could obtain from them. Whaling captains could make fortunes from the whale's blubber and baleen.

Carl Spencer/Earthviews

**Q.** Do people still eat whale meat?

**A.** Some sperm whale meat is still eaten but it is not very tasty. In some places people still chew on sperm whale steaks if nothing better is available. Belly blubber is a delicacy in Iceland, and the Japanese eat raw blubber in hot spicy sauces.

▼ *While the catcher prepares to end the life of a dying whale, smoke rises from the tryworks on the factory ship as the blubber from another whale is boiled.*

Ann Ronan Picture Library

▲ *Men using sharp spades remove the blubber from a dead whale and chop it into smaller pieces before boiling it.*

The blubber was boiled into oil for lighting and lubrication. "Whalebone" (which is not true bone but more like our fingernails) was made from the baleen plates. The hair or fiber was trimmed. The "whalebone" was then softened, trimmed, and shaped and made into stiffening for clothes, whips, and umbrellas.

For more than a century all fashionable people used whale products in their homes. They used "whalebone" in their clothing to make themselves look slimmer, and they used whale oil lamps and whale candles to light their homes.

One large right whale could provide 2 tons of whalebone and 25 tons of oil. If a whaleboat could catch just one large whale, it would pay for all the costs of the voyage and provide hundreds of thousands of dollars in profit.

### Why the sperm whale was hunted

Whaling became an even bigger business when the whaling boats started to hunt sperm whales in the early nineteenth century.

Sperm whale oil was used to make margarine and soap. It was also used as one of the ingredients in the explosive nitroglycerine and in paints. The oil from the spermaceti organ in the sperm whale's head was used to make candles, polishes, pencils, and cosmetics. It could also be used for medical purposes to protect the skin.

Sperm whale oil and the oil from the spermaceti were mixed to make sperm oil. Up to the present day, sperm oil has been used in such things as germicides and detergents.

As well as the oils from the sperm whale, other parts of the body were used. Tendons were used for stringing tennis racquets and as "catgut" by surgeons to sew up wounds. Whale skin was turned into bootlaces, shoes, bicycle saddles, and suitcases. The bones were made into fertilizers, and the tissues were made into glue. Livers were used to make vitamins. Ambergris, a waxy substance from the intestines of sperm whales, was used in love potions and in making perfume.

With all these products to sell it is easy to see how whaling captains became rich.

### Using whales today

Whale products are not used very much today. Whales are now protected species and cannot be killed. Products made from whales can no longer be traded in most countries, and people have now found substitutes.

There are still a few secret independent whalers in the world, but the days when no whale was safe from greedy whalers are over.

"THE DUCHESS" (THOMAS'S PATENT)

SOLE PROPRIETORS.
YOUNG, CARTER, AND OVERALL.

▲ *A nineteenth-century love seat built from whale ribs and carved vertebrae.*

▲ *Baleen in its raw state (above and right) was softened, trimmed, and shaped to provide fashionable products such as corset stays and umbrella ribs, shown in the two advertisements.*

▲ *Whale oil stored in casks awaiting transport to factories where it was made into candles, margarine, soap, or cosmetics.*

## Cutting up the carcass

In the early whaling days, the catcher boat towed the dead whale back to the mother ship. The whale was tied up at the head and tail alongside the mother ship. A line through one of the flippers hauled the carcass out of the water.

Crew members had the dirty and dangerous job of *flensing* (cutting and removing the skin and blubber). In a heavy, rough sea, this was no easy task. The men fitted metal spurs to their seaboots to help them grip the surface of the whale. They used long-handled, very sharp spades to cut the blubber into strips. A hole was cut for a rope and toggle at the start of every strip.

The rope was passed through a heavy tackle fixed to the mast. Men on the deck of the ship pulled on the ropes to peel away the strips of blubber.

When the head was reached, the baleen or whalebone was hacked out from each side. It too was hauled on deck. What was left of the carcass was abandoned to the sea . . . and the hungry sharks.

Back on deck, sailors cut the long strips of blubber into smaller pieces. The pieces of blubber were stored in casks, but the casks had to be packed properly since gases were given off by the decomposing blubber. An exploding cask was not a happy thought.

More modern mother ships had a special "cutting-in-stage" (like a window cleaner's or painter's platform) rigged over the side of the mother or factory ship. This platform, which was fitted with a handrail, made the job less dangerous for the men with the cutting spades.

Later, factory ships took the entire whale on board. Then nobody had to work on a shaky platform over the side of the ship. These ships were true factories. They went to sea to catch whales and returned with a load of oil and other processed whale products ready to sell.

Shore stations were obviously the easiest places to process whales. They had space and plenty of fresh water for steam winches and saws, as well as for cleaning the blood and mess. But best of all, they did not go up and down like a ship in a storm. Life for men at the shore stations was much more pleasant than it was on the factory ships.

▼ *A factory ship, built in the 1920s, had a bow that opened to make it easier to get the dead whales on board.*

◄ *Cutting up a whale lashed to the side of the mother ship was a slippery, dangerous job in rough seas. On land the job was less hazardous because the flensing deck did not go up and down.*

► *The gory job of cutting up whale carcasses was more efficient on shore.*

◄ *A bowhead carcass with cuts already made, ready for the skin to be stripped off. Its long baleen also made the bowhead a target for the whalers.*

▼ *A fin whale being cut up at a shore station in Iceland. Fin whales are threatened by illegal hunting and ocean pollution.*

# Protecting whales

By the late nineteenth century, whaling had become so efficient that the whales did not stand a chance. Many species had been hunted until only a few were left. Some species were almost extinct. People began to get worried. Did we really want a world without whales?

## The first attempts at protection

The whalers themselves were the first to realize that some species were almost extinct. It became very difficult to find a single humpback, blue, right, or sperm whale to hunt. Modern technology, shore-based stations and efficient factory ships had almost cleared some parts of the world's oceans of whales. But still the whales were hunted.

In 1911, the British Museum (Natural History) called for scientific research into the mass killing of Antarctic whales, especially humpbacks. This research found that numbers were now very low. Scientists demanded protection around the world. International committees discussed the problem. Reports were published. But still the slaughter continued.

The problem was that commercial whaling was big business. Many countries earned a lot of money from whaling, and most of them were unwilling to just give up that wealth without a struggle. When the League of Nations produced a convention to regulate whaling, nothing happened. Some countries refused to obey the new regulations, and there was no law that could force them to.

**Q.** Has all whale killing stopped?

**A.** No. Some countries like Norway, Japan, Iceland, and Korea continue whaling for scientific purposes. The IWC allows this so that information on reproduction, age, and other details can be obtained. Many people still feel that too many whales are killed since observation rather than killing would provide the same information. The Eskimos are also allowed to hunt 20–30 whales each year. They have hunted whales for centuries, and catching whales is part of their way of life.

▼ *Now idle, this shore station on a barren subantarctic island was known as "the slum of the Southern Ocean" to the men on the whaling ships.*

*The logo of the International Whaling Commission (IWC), which has done much to protect whales since 1946.*

The International Council for the Exploration of the Sea was a little more successful in 1945. It pointed out that young, immature whales needed protection, especially the almost extinct humpbacks. It was agreed that hunting from factory ships should be limited and the length of the catching season shortened. It did not stop whaling but it did try to limit the number of whales that could be killed each year. A whale sanctuary was also established and an inspector appointed.

## International Whaling Commission

The greatest hope for saving whales came in 1946 when the International Whaling Commission (IWC) was formed. The aim of the IWC was to protect the future of whales. It set *quotas* on the number of whales that could be caught. These quotas limited the number of "blue whale units" each country could catch. A "blue whale unit" was calculated as 1 blue whale = 2 fin whales = 2.5 humpbacks = 6 sei whales.

Unfortunately, this meant that the whalers hunted the largest whale (the blue whale) first. When the blue whales were overhunted they then turned to the fin whales. When the fin whale numbers dropped, they turned to humpbacks. And so it continued until only the minke whales were left in any number.

But gradually protection increased. One species after another was given protection. And one country after another gave up commercial whaling. In 1979, all factory-ship whaling stopped and, finally, in 1986 an "indefinite moratorium" on commercial whaling started. An "indefinite moratorium" means that whaling has stopped at present and no date for starting it again has been decided.

Whaling has not been stopped for ever. If or when it starts again, controlling the number of whales killed will be very important.

▲ *From the now-abandoned Grytviken whaling station, boats set out to slaughter whales.*

▶ *Blue whale*

▼ *Representatives of member nations signing the IWC agreement in Washington, D.C., in November 1946.*

### Did you know?

In one single year (1930), 30,000 blue whales were killed by whalers. Between 1930 and 1940, gray whales became extinct in Asia because of hunting. Humpback whales pass close to land, unlike most other species, so they were hunted almost to extinction from both land and sea.

## Whale numbers today

Technology helped the whalers to become more efficient at killing whales, and it is now helping the IWC and others to count the whales left in the world's oceans.

Aerial surveys tell us where whales are found and how many there are. The table shows the number of whales that we estimate are left in the world's oceans, and the number that we think there were before commercial whaling started. Do you think we have been successful in protecting our whales?

### Estimate of whale numbers

| Species | Before commercial whaling | Now |
|---|---|---|
| Sperm whale | 2,400,000 | 1,950,000 |
| Blue whale | 228,000 | 14,000 |
| Fin whale | 548,000 | 120,000 |
| Sei whale | 256,000 | 54,000 |
| Bryde's whale | 90,000 | 90,000 |
| Minke whale | 576,000 | 505,000 |
| Gray whale | more than 20,000 | 18,000 |
| Right whale | 100,000 | 4,000 |
| Bowhead | 30,000 | 7,200 |
| Humpback | 115,000 | 10,000 |

▲ *Without protection the humpback could have become extinct and this spectacular sight of a humpback breaching would have been lost to us for ever.*

▶ *The bones of a whale left on King George Island are a memorial to the thousands of whales killed in the Antarctic.*

▼ *There are now 10,000 humpbacks left in the world's oceans. Scientists estimate that there were 115,000 before commercial whaling began.*

# Strandings

Most whales found lying on a beach are dead. The whales have died in the sea from disease, old age, or some other cause. A few of these dead whales are washed up each year on beaches around the world. But sometimes live whales will strand, either alone, or in a small group.

### What causes live strandings?

Whales, most of which live well out to sea, do not live-strand as often as dolphins or porpoises, which live closer to land. But a single whale sometimes does strand. As whales live together in small groups, sometimes all the members of the group will strand together.

There have been many theories about what causes live strandings. These include sickness, falling asleep in shallow water, suicide, earthquakes, storms, pollution, or confusion caused by radio and television transmissions. None of these theories can explain all strandings satisfactorily.

Scientists now believe that whales strand because they make a mistake in navigation.

The earth has a geomagnetic field in which there are "hills" (or high points) and "valleys" (or low points). Whales have a magnetic sense, which they use to "read" this field in the same way we would use a map — to tell us in which direction we are going. The whales keep the higher field on one side and the lower field on the other. This is rather like you walking across the slope of a hill with one foot up the hill and one foot down. There are problems, however, near shore. The magnetic "hills" and "valleys" do not end at the beach, they continue onto land and sometimes so do the whales.

Live strandings are like road accidents due to mistakes in map reading. This explains why live stranded animals appear to be shocked and why they need help to leave the beach. They are like shocked passengers after a car crash who need help from passers-by.

Luckily these accidents are rare. There are hundreds of thousands of whales in the sea. They are usually very good at using their map to migrate thousands of miles every year. Very few end up alive on the shore.

### Can we prevent live strandings?

There is little we can do to prevent strandings. Luckily, so few whales strand that there is no threat to the survival of any species. All we can do is care for the shocked and confused whale that has accidentally stranded.

It is possible to refloat smaller species without injury to the rescuers or the whale. However, it is very difficult to refloat a very large stranded whale.

Very heavy equipment is needed but it is not always available. On isolated beaches surrounded by cliffs or rocks it is difficult to get the lifting equipment onto the beach. The huge weight of the whale's body presses on vital organs, such as the lungs, and damages them when it is stranded on land. Often a whale expert must kill the animal to prevent further pain and distress.

▼ *Humpbacks migrate long distances every year from their winter breeding grounds to their summer feeding grounds. Live strandings on these journeys are very rare.*

▲ *Most whales, such as this sperm whale, are already dead when they are found washed up on the shore.*

Jonathan Player/Ardea London

### Did you know?

Whales often make their navigational mistake one or even two days before they actually strand. When the whale "reads" its map wrongly it continues to go the wrong way until it reaches the shore. Only then does it realize it has made a mistake.

# Helping a stranded whale

If you are alone when you see a whale, there are five things you can do:

1. Try to stay calm and think clearly.
2. Report the stranding to a police officer, lifeguard, teacher, the Coast Guard, or even the tourist information office.
3. Do not get too close to the whale. The tail may suddenly move and knock you over. Or the whale may roll on top of you.
4. Find out whether the animal is alive or dead. This is usually obvious. The animal is either moving or already decaying. If you are not sure, stand well in front of it. Listen for breathing. See if the eyes are open.
5. The most important thing for you to do is to get help quickly.

## When help arrives

The three most important things for helpers to do are as follows:

1. Keep the whale cool, calm, and comfortable, if it is alive.
2. Record accurate details and measurements, whether the whale is alive or dead.
3. Get expert help as soon as possible.

Whales are built for the water. They quickly overheat on land. It is most important to keep the flippers, fin, and tail cool. The whale's skin is delicate and dries out quickly. Keep the skin damp with wet sacks, sheets, or buckets of water. Do not get water or sand in the blowhole — water in the blowhole can drown the whale; sand can damage the lungs.

The whale will be shocked and distressed. All helpers should stay calm and soothe it.

Record accurate details with photographs or sketches. Experts will need to know what size the whale is. They will need a good description to decide what species it is. They also need to know exactly where it is lying.

It is often a good idea to split helpers into teams. One team can fetch water for cooling the whale. One team can keep bystanders away. One team can record details and note measurements. One team can soothe the whale. One team should look after the helpers, who are going to be tired, cold, and hungry.

When an expert arrives he or she will take responsibility. Only an expert can decide how or if a whale can be returned to the water or whether the animal is in great pain and must be destroyed.

Stephen Leatherwood/Earthviews

▲ *Whales that pass close to shore are more likely to live-strand than whales that spend their lives far out to sea.*

# Q. Why do scientists not know everything about why whales strand?

# A. Because whales are not easy animals to study. Studying them in the wild is difficult, and dead whales cannot provide all the answers. It is difficult to find out how organs work when the whale is dead (and often decomposed) and the organs have stopped working.

▼ *It is very difficult to refloat a large stranded whale like this one. Built for a life in water, the weight of its body often damages vital organs, and humane killing by an expert is often the only solution.*

Craig Matkin/Earthviews

# Race to free trapped whales

Sometimes humans are able to help whales that have stranded on shore. In October 1988, humans were also able to help three California gray whales that had been trapped by ice in the cold Alaskan waters.

## October 7, 1988
Three California gray whales become trapped under the ice in the frozen waters of Alaska while they are migrating south to warmer waters to breed. Some time later they are discovered by Inupiat Eskimos from a nearby village. The Eskimos cut two small breathing holes in the ice.

## October 19
Bones, Crossbeak, and Bonnet — the nicknamed whales — are bleeding and battered from hitting their heads on the jagged ice. They are exhausted from swimming against the ocean current to stay near the breathing holes. They are threatened by attack from polar bears who are running across the ice, attracted by the scent of blood. One whale has symptoms of pneumonia.

## October 20
An ice-breaking barge heading to help the whales is delayed after it gets stuck in ice. The Eskimos cut new breathing holes for the whales.

## October 22
Radio, television, and newspapers bring the plight of the whales to the attention of the world. International rescue efforts are organized.

## October 24
Bones, the youngest and smallest of the whales, is supported by one of the larger whales at the surface. But after some time it is no longer seen and is presumed dead.

## October 25
An 11-ton ice-breaking machine arrives at the scene. It is so big it has to be flown in aboard the US Air Force C5 Galaxy — the largest aircraft in the world. The United States requests the help of Soviet icebreakers.

## October 26
The weary whales try to go in the wrong direction. Efforts to coax the whales toward open water fail. They must make their way through a 30-foot (9 m) ice ridge if they are to reach a pathway to the sea.

## October 27
Two Soviet icebreakers arrive.

## October 28
The icebreakers open a path to the sea for the two surviving whales. At about 4 p.m., Crossbeak and Bonnet leave the last string of breathing holes cut in the ice, swim 380 yards (350 m) beneath the ice and push their way through slush and ice to swim up the channel in the wake of the Soviet icebreaker. There are no more obstacles in their way to the freedom of the North Pacific.

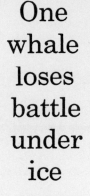

# One whale loses battle under ice

## ALASKA

BARROW (Alaska), Sunday: The youngest and smallest of three stranded California grey whales has died just as efforts to save them appeared to be making significant progress.

When last seen late on Friday night, the whale appeared to be literally riding on the back of one of the other two, its snout so battered that a bare bone poked through as it fought its last battle.

The whales were always together, surfacing as a trio, but by yesterday morning, only two remained and it is presumed that the small whale has drowned — exhausted, bloodied and bruised from its two-week ordeal.

Mr David E. Withrow, a whale expert with the National Marine Mammal Laboratory in Seattle, said the lost whale was probably only about a year old, based on its estimated length of 8.2 to 8.8 metres. The others are around 10.5 metres long, suggesting they are "two, possibly three years old", and appeared to be in good shape.

Eskimo rescuers successfully cut the first series of breathing holes in the ice late on Friday and the whales were swimming from hole to hole.

As soon as each hole was cut, the whales swam to it, checked it out, and then went back to the last hole cut Thursday night.

That hole, about 800 metres from where the whales were discovered two weeks ago, was equipped with a de-icing machine to which the whales are attracted, possibly because of its humming sound.

By sunrise, the Eskimos had created about six holes. The plan is to add more holes and move the de-icer forward, luring the whales with it.

That strategy, which the Eskimos came up with after all sorts of high-tech attempts had failed, appears to be the only chance for survival for the whales.

If the weather holds, the Eskimos could complete a series of holes by today to join those being poked through the ice near open water by an Alaska National Guard helicopter.

Los Angeles Times

Scope Features (Aust)

# Whale tales

In fairy tales wolves are usually villains. Cuddly rabbits are usually heroes. But what is the whale? A villain or a hero? Some of the stories told in this chapter cast the whale as a hero. Whales, after all, are gentle creatures that do not attack or harm humans. Other stories show whales as frightening monsters because they are so much larger than we are.

▶ *Captain Ahab's ship, the* Pequod, *bears down on one of the catcher boats where a member of the crew is about to harpoon a whale.*

### Jonah and the whale

One of the best-known stories about whales comes from the Bible.

Jonah disobeyed God's orders to go to the city of Nineveh to preach against the wickedness of its citizens. The ship he was on got caught in a violent storm. The crew decided that Jonah had caused the storm and threw him into the sea, where he was swallowed by a whale. Jonah spent three days and nights in the whale's stomach. Finally, the whale spat Jonah onto land. Jonah hurried to Nineveh as God had ordered. The sinful Ninevites repented, and God spared the city. The whale was certainly God's chosen creature in this story.

### The whale and the sea slug

One of Aesop's fables tells the story of the hare and the tortoise. A story with a similar theme also appears in Japanese folklore.

Once upon a time there was a boastful monster whale and a small, but clever, sea slug. The whale boasted that he was the greatest animal in the sea and challenged the sea slug to a race. They agreed to hold the race in three days' time.

The sea slug asked each of his sea slug friends to travel to a different beach and wait for the whale. The day of the race arrived. The monster whale sped off into the sea. The sea slug followed slowly behind him.

At the beach, which was supposed to be the end of the race, the whale called out, "Sea slug, where are you?" The waiting sea slug called back, "What, whale? Have you only just arrived?" (All this was said in Japanese, of course). The sea slug suggested that they race again to another beach, and off they set.

The whale arrived at the second beach and called, "Sea slug, where are you?" The waiting sea slug replied "What, whale? Have you only just arrived?" The race continued but at every beach the result was the same. Finally, the exhausted whale admitted defeat. He never boasted again.

▲ *With little knowledge of the anatomy of a whale, artists in the past used their vivid imaginations and drew whales as monsters with scaly skins, chimneys instead of blowholes, and tusks instead of baleen.*

▼ *This Japanese print, painted in 1851, shows a stranded whale.*

## Moby Dick

The treachery of humans and their killing of whales grew after the whaling industry started in the fifteenth century. But the most famous whaling story, *Moby Dick* by Herman Melville, was written only 150 years ago.

*Moby Dick* tells the story of Captain Ahab and his revenge against the whale that had caused him to lose a leg. The leg he lost had been replaced by a gleaming ivory jaw, but Ahab did not lose his desire for revenge.

On a cold Christmas Day, the whaler *Pequod* "blindly plunged like fate into the lone Atlantic." The search for Moby Dick is long and full of adventure. Finally, they sight the whale, and the chase begins.

Ahab battles with Moby Dick for three days using a special harpoon edged with razors. His huge body writhing with the pain from embedded harpoons, Moby Dick rams the boats lowered from the *Pequod*. The sea is a boiling mass of half-drowned sailors, tangled lines, and sinking boats.

On the third day Moby Dick rams the *Pequod* itself, and Ahab harpoons the whale for the last time. As the whale thrashes in the sea and dies, Ahab gets caught in the rope from the harpoon. He is sucked into the sea and drowns.

Moby Dick may not have been the hero of this story but he was certainly not as great a villain as Captain Ahab.

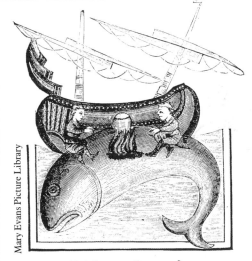

### Did you know?

Many centuries ago there were stories of sailors mistaking whales for islands. They would anchor their boat off the "island" and step onto the "land." Lighting a fire to cook food they were rather surprised when the sleeping whale, feeling the heat from the fire, dived beneath the water, taking the sailors and their dinner with it.

# Glossary

BALEEN — Plates of horny fiber arranged on both sides of the whale's upper jaw. It is used to sieve or filter small crustaceans from the water.

BLOW — A moist, usually white, vapor that is blown up into the air, when a whale breathes out. The blow or spout can be seen from a great distance in clear weather.

BLOWHOLE — Nostril on the top of a whale's head through which it breathes. Baleen whales have two blowholes or nostrils. Sperm whales, dolphins, and porpoises have only one blowhole.

BLUBBER — The layer of fat found between the skin and muscle of whales and from which oil is extracted

CALLOSITIES — Hard, thick parts of the skin, which look like large raised warts. Northern and southern right whales have callosities on their jaws and head where lice attach.

CATCHER (BOAT) — The boat from which a whale is actually harpooned. This was often a small open boat launched from a larger ship. The men in the catcher boats were called catchers.

CROW'S NEST — A box or shelter used by the lookout, near the top of a ship's mast.

CRUSTACEANS — Any of a number of species with no backbone, with a hard outside shell or crust, and jointed limbs. Most crustaceans — like crabs, lobsters, and shrimps — live in the water.

DORSAL FIN — A fin that stands upright on the back of many species of whale and other marine animals, such as sharks. The dorsal fins of whales are usually small, and triangular or slightly hooked. The dorsal fin helps the whale to steer.

FLENSING — Stripping the blubber and skin from a whale.

FLIPPERS — The two broad flat limbs that a whale has, one on either side of its body instead of arms. The flippers are used for steering and balance when the whale is swimming.

FLUKES — The two triangular lobes or parts of a whale's tail. The flukes beat up and down to move the whale through the water.

FOSSILS — The remains (usually bones and teeth) of animals (or plants), belonging to past ages, and found buried in the earth.

HAREM — Originally a harem was the part of an oriental palace reserved for women only, all of whom "belonged" to one man. A bull whale's harem describes the group of female whales that one bull (or sometimes two bulls) mate with, not allowing any other bulls to approach.

KRILL — The word krill is a collective name used to describe a number of shrimp-like crustaceans, which are the main food of baleen whales.

MAMMAL — An animal with a backbone whose young feed upon milk from the mother's breasts. Most mammals, except whales, have hair, all have a diaphragm for breathing and most give birth to live young rather than laying eggs (except for the platypus and the echidna of Australia).

MOTHER SHIP — A large ship, which looked after or "mothered" a number of smaller catcher boats launched from its decks. The mother ship was home to all the crew until the whales were spotted. Then the crew had the job of launching the catcher boats and dealing with the dead whales brought back by the catchers.

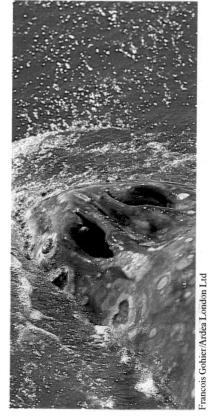

Ben Osborne/Oxford Scientific Films

Dave Watts/Australasian Nature Transparencies

Mike Osmond

| ORDER | A large scientific group. Whales belong to the order Cetacea. |
|---|---|
| PARASITES | Animals or plants that live on and get their food from the body of another animal or plant, called the host. Parasites often damage their hosts. Although they live on the whale's body, whale "parasites" are often not true parasites because they get their food from scraps in the water around the whale, not from its body. |
| QUOTA | The largest amount of something that a country is allowed to produce and sell. International Whaling Commission quotas limited the number of whales that each member country could kill each year. |
| SPECIES | A group of animals or plants with common characteristics, capable of breeding with others in the group but not usually outside it. The species is the basic unit of scientific classification or sorting. |
| SPERMACETI ORGAN | A large structure inside the sperm whale's head that contains a white, fatty, waxy substance. Spermaceti "oil" was used to make candles, ointments, and cosmetics. |
| STRAND | To find yourself stuck somewhere you do not want to be with no resources to help you. In the case of a whale it means to run onto the shore accidentally. |
| VERTEBRAE | Small bones that make up the spine. An animal with vertebrae is called a vertebrate. |
| WHALEBONE | Another name for baleen, which in fact is more like horn or human fingernails than bone. |
| WHALER | A boat used for hunting whales or a person who hunts whales. |

## List of scientific names

| Common Name | Scientific Name |
|---|---|
| blue whale | *Balaenoptera musculus* |
| bowhead | *Balaena mysticetus* |
| Bryde's whale | *Balaenoptera edeni* |
| dwarf sperm whale | *Kogia simus* |
| fin whale | *Balaenoptera physalus* |
| gray whale | *Eschrichtius robustus* |
| humpback | *Megaptera novaeangliae* |
| minke whale | *Balaenoptera acutorostrata* |
| northern right whale | *Eubalaena glacialis* |
| pygmy right whale | *Caperea marginata* |
| pygmy sperm whale | *Kogia breviceps* |
| sei whale | *Balaenoptera borealis* |
| southern right whale | *Eubalaena australis* |
| sperm whale | *Physeter catodon* |

# Index

Paul Er...

Al Giddings/Ocean Images, Inc./Planet Earth Pictures

G.L. K...